Guide to Classifying INDUSTRIAL PROPERTY

SECOND EDITION

Johannson L. Yap
Rene M. Circ

ULI

Urban Land Institute

Recommended bibliographic listing:

Yap, Johannson L., and Rene M. Circ. *Guide to Classifying Industrial Property.* Second Edition. Washington, D.C.: ULI–the Urban Land Institute, 2003.

ULI Catalog Number: G12
International Standard Book Number: 0-87420-895-5
Library of Congress Control Number: 2003102379

1025 Thomas Jefferson Street, N.W.
Suite 500 West
Washington, D.C. 20007-5201

PROJECT STAFF

Rachelle L. Levitt
Senior Vice President, Policy and Practice
Publisher

Gayle Berens
Vice President, Real Estate Development Practice

Anne B. Frej
Director, Office and Industrial Development
Project Director

Nancy H. Stewart
Director, Book Program
Managing Editor

Laura Glassman, Publications Professionals LLC
Copy Editor

Betsy VanBuskirk
Art Director
Book Design

Helene Y. Redmond/HYR Graphics
Design/Layout/Cover Design

Diann Stanley-Austin
Director, Publishing Operations

ABOUT ULI–THE URBAN LAND INSTITUTE

ULI–the Urban Land Institute is a nonprofit education and research institute that is supported by its members. Its mission is to provide responsible leadership in the use of land in order to enhance the total environment.

ULI sponsors education programs and forums to encourage an open international exchange of ideas and sharing of experiences; initiates research that anticipates emerging land use trends and issues and proposes creative solutions based on that research; provides advisory services; and publishes a wide variety of materials to disseminate information on land use and development. Established in 1936, the Institute today has more than 18,000 members and associates from some 60 countries representing the entire spectrum of the land use and development disciplines.

Richard M. Rosan
President

ABOUT FIRST INDUSTRIAL REALTY TRUST, INC.

First Industrial Realty Trust, Inc., is the nation's largest provider of diversified industrial real estate. The company has extensive experience building, buying, selling, leasing, and managing diverse industrial facility types in major industrial markets throughout the United States.

A focus on industrial property enables First Industrial to provide expertise on a broad range of industrial property issues. By specializing in diverse facility types, the company is uniquely prepared to serve each critical component of a client's distribution network in any of the strategic markets in which it operates. First Industrial's properties are managed by local employees who provide exceptional service to the company's customers and can respond promptly to market opportunities around the nation.

In response to the complex needs of corporate America, First Industrial offers Integrated Industrial Solutions™ (IIS™), a fully integrated portfolio of services organized to provide complete solutions to industrial real estate needs, including: build-to-suit development, redevelopment, industrial facility leasing, single tenant/user sales, sale/leaseback transactions, and surplus property acquisitions. Through this program, the company leverages its operating platform and employee expertise to deliver comprehensive solutions to complex, multimarket supply chain reconfiguration needs.

Michael W. Brennan
President and Chief Executive Officer

ACKNOWLEDGMENTS

The *Guide to Classifying Industrial Property* was first conceived by First Industrial Realty Trust as a resource to explain the diversity of industrial real estate to its customers and others involved in industrial development and investment. Because of the positive response to the first edition produced by First Industrial and the recognition that the book fills an important gap in the classification of industrial properties, a decision was made to publish a second edition. This edition is the result of a collaboration between First Industrial Realty Trust and ULI–the Urban Land Institute to make the publication available to a wide audience.

Many individuals and organizations were instrumental in providing information and assisting in the creation of the book, particularly in its early phases. Mike Brennan, president and chief executive officer of First Industrial Realty Trust, Inc., provided counsel and encouragement throughout the process. First Industrial field members also contributed information and local market expertise covering 25 major industrial markets across the country. Special recognition goes to the company's senior management who reviewed and commented on the book.

Other professionals furnished useful suggestions that were incorporated. Ken Ackerman of Warehousing Forum, Mike Jones of St. Onge Company, and Steve Laposa of PricewaterhouseCoopers supplied guidance as well as important technical information in the area of logistics and supply chain management. Jim DeLisle at the University of Washington assisted with the first edition and also contributed the foreword to the current edition. Kord Williams, Northwest Airlines, provided plans of air cargo and airport hangar buildings. SSI-Schäfer-Noell GmbH provided plans and pictures of rack-supported warehouses. Steve Saunders of Eckenhoff Saunders Associates and Mark Leszczewicz of Alliance Insurance Company provided useful background information. Thanks go to Mark Hassinger of Lerner Development Group and to David Twist of AMB Property Corporation for reviewing the manuscript of the latest version of the book and offering their insights into industrial property trends.

Anne Frej, director, office and industrial development, at the Urban Land Institute, was instrumental in producing the current revised edition of *Guide to Classifying Industrial Property*. Her ideas for revisions and additional information resulted in an improved, updated book. Rachelle Levitt, senior vice president, policy and practice, and Gayle Berens, vice president, real estate development practice, at ULI also provided important advice and encouragement.

Victoria J. Baker edited the first version, and Laura Glassman edited the current edition, with the editing/production process guided by Nancy Stewart. The original design and graphics were coordinated by BHI Design. Betsy VanBuskirk and Helene Redmond created the final design.

Johannson L. Yap
Rene M. Circ
First Industrial Realty Trust, Inc.
Chicago, Illinois

CONTENTS

FOREWORD

NEED FOR THE BOOK

This book plays an important role in the evolution of institutional real estate by presenting a more precise classification system for industrial properties than is currently available. This added precision is an important building block as investors and portfolio managers, as well as developers, search for new, sustainable opportunities in a rapidly changing marketplace and as space users look for optimal real estate solutions. Access to standardized definitions that provide more accurate measures of the risk-return characteristics of various industrial real estate products is critical for investors seeking to capture attractive risk-adjusted returns. With this insight, they should be able to make better industrial allocation decisions relative to other property types. These data can also help investors exploit inefficiencies in the market by allowing them to refine their industrial investment strategies based on the knowledge that different industrial categories react to different market forces. For developers, more precise definitions of industrial property types will help them match physical product to tenant demand, thereby improving the marketability of investments. They can offer better-customized solutions that appeal to tenants with specialized needs without incurring costs for unnecessary features. For users, the ability to select real estate offerings that best fit their specific needs over a specific time horizon offers the opportunity for enhanced productivity and corporate earnings.

INCREASINGLY DYNAMIC MARKETPLACE

Some institutional investors and developers view warehouse properties as relatively safe, bond-type investments, generating competitive returns with moderate risk exposures. Indeed, over the long term, the industrial sector has tended to provide more stable risk-adjusted returns than some of the more dynamic property types—such as office, retail, or hotel—for investors with core strategies that are managed relatively passively. Despite such experience, however, there is no reason to think this competitive advantage will hold in the future, because the industrial real estate market has been subject to structural changes in space demand, changes in manufacturing and distribution channels, and growing product diversity in terms of physical and locational elements. The end result is the need to approach industrial real estate development and investment in a much more strategic, proactive manner to ensure continued success. Finally, the opportunity to tap into the sector's potential has been made practical and cost-effective by advances in knowledge management and data mining that make it easier to exploit inefficiencies in the market.

STRUCTURAL CHANGES IN SPATIAL DEMAND

Changes in the demand for industrial space that have occurred over the past decade can be attributed to factors such as improved production processes; advances in productivity due to automation and computer-aided design and manufacturing; and improved inventory tracking and forecasting techniques. Because many of these changes are more revolutionary than evolutionary, it is impossible to rely on past industry trends and emerging patterns to predict and anticipate future outcomes and effects on real estate. Thus, quantitative, time-series-type trend analysis must be supplemented with a more qualitative approach that takes structural changes into consideration, especially since those changes have not been distributed equally across various segments of the industrial market and have created market inefficiencies as a result of uninformed, risk-averse strategies. For example, the fear of being stuck with unmarketable space has forced many institutional investors to adopt a risk-management strategy that restricts investments to modern, state-of-the-art facilities. Although this approach might appear to be prudent, actually it can lead to a capital-driven mismatch in which developers overbuild or overimprove industrial facilities relative to tenant demand. Since reactions to structural forces vary widely by type of tenant, the strategy of concentrating on "modern" facilities to avoid being stuck with functionally obsolescent investments creates a false sense of security. Without recognizing the specialized spatial needs of various demand segments, developers and investors may incorrectly opt for industrial properties that are theoretically appealing to a wide audience but have limited demand. This possibility is especially likely when investment policies ignore the role that a particular market plays in the broader manufacturing and distribution system. Finally, the bottom-line focus of many companies in the new economy has amplified the demand for more specialized, customized solutions. Knowing how to classify a "unique" property can promote a solution permitting conversion of the property to alternative uses without requiring investment of massive capital for renovation. Thus, the space-time component can be compressed without excessive capital expenses. Added precision in categorizing industrial real estate can allow developers and investors to build, design, and buy better products that have locked-in clients, creating an oligopolistic advantage facing less competition than do those who approach the sector with the attitude that one size should fit all.

In addition to seeking knowledge on changing spatial requirements, investors and developers should develop better techniques for making decisions regarding industrial real estate. Relying on such insight, analysts can better predict real estate needs measured in space-time and money-time terms that recognize the costs and challenges associated with changing real estate options. For example, although analysis of a tenant's spatial needs might argue for moving to a property more compatible with corporate needs, existing lease terms, financial resources, decision-making models, and other factors might prevent or defer such a choice. In another scenario, consolidation of two companies will ultimately result in divestiture of assets, with some decisions more driven by which party is the acquiring interest and which corporate culture dominates rather than by more objective measures of space needs or business process fit. Bankruptcies and forced restructuring also can create a situation in which the occupancy or tenancy of individual investments or groups of investments can be wiped out in an unexpected manner. The failure to understand the underlying business of tenants, both existing and potential, could undercut the creditworthy nature of a portfolio of space, subject it to systemic risk when a particular sector (e.g., technology or telecommunications) or a company (e.g., Enron, Consolidated Freightways) implodes, or both. Although such wipeouts caused by external forces cannot be foreseen, investors and developers can manage their severity through diversification strategies that reduce reliance on demand segments subject to systemic risk. Such strategies should allow developers and investors to avoid being left holding functionally obsolescent space for which there is limited or no effective demand. By understanding the business processes of key tenant groups, real estate managers should be able to develop more strategic relationships with tenants, leading to greater collaboration and vertical integration of services.

GROWING PRODUCT DIVERSITY

The supply function for warehouse facilities has dramatically changed, both in terms of their development and ownership structure and in terms of physical assets. For example, because of the relatively short time needed to construct new facilities and the relatively low cost of carrying "entitled" property on the books, developers typically waited for tenant commitments before building new facilities. Often, these developers were local players, who controlled the relatively limited supply of industrial land. This supply-side elasticity was one of the saving factors over recent business cycles, allowing the industrial sector to respond quickly to increases in supply. Over the past decade, in many markets the profile of industrial developers has changed to large, well-capitalized, regional or national players. These new players, both public and private, have demonstrated a willingness to take on greater development risk and add speculative building products to the market. This strategy has resulted in overbuilding cycles that are more frequent and of higher magnitude than previous long-term averages for the industrial property sector.

FOREWORD

More savvy developers and investors who have been able to gain greater insight into tenant demand and industry trends have moved into the development of more-specialized facilities. As a result, the array of industrial products has increased, creating a potpourri of investment and development opportunities. This product diversity is expected to expand even more, as space users seek to improve efficiency and productivity to remain competitive in an increasingly sophisticated and dynamic business environment. These changes make the major industrial categories historically used (e.g., warehouse, manufacturing, and research and development [R&D]) too broad to provide meaningful insight into the composition of the overall industrial market. Although most industrial properties can indeed be rolled into those three major groupings, they are simply too diverse to be treated as conglomerated sectors. Within those major categories a wide array of subtypes are subject to significantly different drivers of value and market functions. Without an understanding of those differences, analysts and investors cannot accurately determine market balance and may falsely interpret signals of the relative balance of supply and demand. For example, although overall warehouse space may be in an oversaturated state in a particular market, critical shortages may exist within specialized subcategories. The product cycles for various industrial strata can differ widely. These cyclical differences are the result of issues on the production side, as in the case of barriers to entry for large facilities and high costs of capital associated with specialized facilities that create prolonged development phases, capital constraints, or both.

INCREASED RESEARCH BENEFITS

Understanding the increasingly segmented demand and supply side of the industrial sector is a daunting task. However, market changes have rendered passive approaches that focus only on certain core industrial assets obsolete in assessing risk/return tradeoffs. A generalized approach to industrial development and investment can still be profitable, but it will be inferior to more strategic approaches that respond to rapidly changing market needs that arise from broad business trends and supply-chain reconfiguration.

The good news for those dealing in the industrial sector is that the real estate market has become more efficient in terms of information access and analytical processes. To some extent, the availability of more-specialized data has been caused by the emergence of the public side of the market, such as real estate investment trusts (REITs) and commercial mortgage–based securities (CMBS). At the same time, the Internet and other technological innovations have created an explosion in the volume and accessibility of data about real estate and markets. The availability of such data, coupled with improvements in the tools by which they can be accessed and analyzed (e.g., relational databases, statistical models, geographic information systems), has made more informed decision making possible. One of the prerequisites to take advantage of such advances is the ability to disaggregate the overall industrial sector into meaningful classes for which such data can be compiled, analyzed, and disseminated through trade associations and third-party vendors. Using more specific data, investors are able to develop more refined investment strategies that outperform more general approaches.

In addition to enhancing industrywide performance for developers and investors through improved access to more precise public information on industrial sectors, a more sophisticated classification system can assist larger investors, managers, or associations who utilize proprietary space-time, money-time data as tools to outperform the broader market. When these data are mapped into meaningful industrial classes, data management, data mining, and data analysis tools can be used to develop investment strategies that exploit informational inefficiencies—especially in the industrial sector, in which many passive investors are content to focus on mainstream, core properties, markets, and tenants. Investors and managers gain an understanding of their existing clientele and operational efficiencies, as well as the ability to identify new initiatives and niches that will firm up their competitive advantage and open new frontiers.

CLASSIFICATION REQUIREMENTS

In recent years, the need for a more precise, unambiguous classification system for industrial properties has become clear. The necessary level of detail for such a system hinges on several key considerations that can help strike a balance between too few and too many categories.

- First, the categories should comprise comparable assets that share fundamental physical elements differentiating them from other classes in terms of physical and spatial attributes.
- Second, each of the classes must have distinct market processes of supply, demand, and investment that apply to the spatial side of the equation in terms of supply/demand interaction, as well as to the capital side of the equation in terms of price setting and investor appeal.
- Third, the groupings must be meaningful, sharing underlying commonalities that affect investment performance. Ultimately, these effects should distinguish risk/return profiles, be measurable, and be predictable. In addition, the categories should be meaningful in that the market will be rewarded for understanding and incorporating their unique character in terms of performance, either individually or collectively.
- Fourth, the classification system should be comprehensive, embracing the full array of properties that fall under the broad industrial label.
- Fifth, the classes must be substantial, as measured in terms of market size and investment opportunities. That is, each of the classes must comprehend a significant level of wealth. In addition to size, each category must include a number of investment opportunities for which there is a positive cost-benefit tradeoff for the added rigor associated with understanding the nuances of the asset class. Given the capital-intensive nature of real estate, this consideration is particularly important because decision makers must live with their choices over time in the face of an increasingly sophisticated and dynamic business environment.
- Finally, the classification system must be reliable, capable of accurately grouping components over a reasonable forecast period. This criterion is important to avoid a continuously changing system that thwarts the collection of time-series data needed to provide insights into prior performance and serve as a basis for predicted performance.

INVESTMENT CONSIDERATIONS

An exploration of the portfolio management process illustrates the importance of the classification system presented in this book. Most institutional investors view industrial investments as a subset of a larger real estate portfolio—which, in turn, is a component of a broader mixed-asset portfolio. Real estate investments typically constitute a portion of a mixed-asset portfolio that includes other asset classes such as stocks and bonds. For investors, superior performance and diversification are important considerations in portfolio management. Because real estate has a relatively low correlation with other asset classes, it provides diversification benefits that can help stabilize overall portfolio returns. In the case of mixed-asset portfolios, investors develop strategies for each of the relatively broad asset classes that provide the overall framework within which individual sectors are managed, as well as guidelines for the selection of individual companies or investment products.

FOREWORD

In managing real estate portfolios, many investors follow a process similar to that applied to the mixed-asset portfolio; however, the extent to which strategic overlays guide portfolio construction and management varies among investors. There are two competing approaches to real estate portfolio management. The *bottom-up* approach focuses on individual assets, ensuring that they exhibit solid fundamentals in terms of size, quality, market, and location. The *top-down* perspective focuses on ensuring that a proper mix of assets is maintained among property types and markets. Today, it is increasingly clear that a hybrid approach is necessary to maximize risk-adjusted returns over the long term. A meaningful classification system can help straddle the two approaches, permitting top-down investors to develop more sophisticated asset allocation strategies and allowing bottom-up investors to develop sector-specific policies that draw on experience to guide individual investment decisions.

In recognition of the importance of diversification, most institutional real estate portfolios contain asset allocations for the major property classes. In the current market, a typical real estate portfolio would consist of 30 to 40 percent office assets, 20 to 30 percent retail, 10 to 20 percent industrial, 10 to 20 percent apartment, and 10 to 20 percent other assets (e.g., international, hotel, timber, agriculture). After establishing this general framework, investors would then develop sector-specific strategies that addressed subsector allocations (e.g., retail allocated among neighborhood, community, regional, and super-regional malls) based on some understanding or expectation for relative performance on a risk-adjusted basis.

The industrial sector label traditionally has covered three subclasses of properties: warehouse, manufacturing, and R&D. Many private investors limit the scope of core institutional–grade industrial properties that will be considered for inclusion in their portfolio to the warehouse and light manufacturing categories. They focus on core industrial space that is sufficiently generic to suit a variety of users, believing this strategy helps avoid getting caught with unique, specialized facilities that either have a very narrow appeal in terms of tenancy or require additional capital expenditures that cannot be amortized over the life of the initial tenancy. Investors also categorize core industrial investments on the basis of office finish and physical design (e.g., ceiling height, loading dock heights, divisibility). For example, some institutional investors define core industrial as properties with high ceiling heights (i.e., 24 to 30 feet), dock-high loading, low office finish (i.e., less than 10 percent), situated in business parks or industrial zones. This additional layer of criteria is intended to help avoid properties that are functionally obsolescent and cannot meet the needs of future tenants. Similarly, many institutional investors tend to avoid R&D properties, the label attached to a wide range of office showroom and customized high-tech, corporate campus–type facilities. As with other specialized facilities, R&D properties are considered specialized, hybrid investments that combine office and warehouse or office and showroom uses in one structure, which should be approached opportunistically to offset higher acquisition costs, narrower tenant appeal, and limited exit strategies.

The core/noncore allocation embraced by many risk-averse institutional investors can backfire in terms of portfolio-level performance. Assuming industrial portfolios are of sufficient scale in terms of number and value of properties, a proactive approach can be used to shift the classification of industrial investments from the noncore to the core category. For example, by careful research and data mining (i.e., tracking what works and what does not) to identify indirect benefits (e.g., lower turnover, higher marginal rent to reward customized space, conversion costs, leading indicators), owners can reduce the risk of noncore activities. In effect, they can use "insider information"—still legal in the inefficient real estate market—to beat the market. In addition, by approaching industrial investments with greater precision and using scale to its advantage, an investor can experiment with various customized portfolio solutions and test what works and what does not work without jeopardizing the whole. For example, investors can strategically allocate a portion of the industrial category to more noncore, opportunistic activities that have a higher risk/higher return profile than bread-and-butter operations. This strategy will allow them to capture potentially higher portfolio-level returns without a commensurate increase in risk. Over time, insights gleaned from actual performance can be used to shift assets from the noncore to the core category. This benefit also applies to market timing, since investors and developers tapping into such proprietary market knowledge can anticipate changes in demand on the margin for various subsectors, allowing them to sell into a softening stage and buy into a recovering one. Those who use generic, unsophisticated approaches that do not recognize the dynamics of demand and supply embedded in the industrial sector will lag behind these more sophisticated, strategic players. Because fiduciary relationships are generally involved in private sector institutional investing, with advisers and consultants providing such a role, it is likely that "best practices" will demand a more precise approach to the industrial sector.

Investors use REITs to fill or supplement their real estate portfolios in an attempt to take more strategic approaches to various property sectors, including the industrial sector. In effect, these investors are using a "risk-management by transfer" mechanism to reduce risk associated with dynamic real estate markets without giving up the potential benefits that can be garnered from a more precise, proactive approach to industrial investments or taking on unmanageable networks of staff or consultants. REITs provide the advantage of centralized management, economies of scale, and a focus on the industrial sector as a means of exploiting potential market inefficiencies created by the broader industry's reliance on generalized approaches. As the market becomes more refined and as investor expectations increase, a more detailed approach to the industrial sector, as supported by the classification system presented in this book, will become increasingly important. Two recent changes have highlighted this need. First, the imposition of greater accountability for corporate executives in other sectors has raised the bar in terms of disclosures for REITs. In order to provide supportable, defensible predictions for performance, managers will have to develop more empirically based outlooks. Second, growing concern over analysts' forecasts and possible conflicts of interest has resulted in new requirements that Wall Street analysts track and report their company ratings against actual performance. Both of these structural changes will force added discipline on those involved in the public real estate market, including the adoption of a more precise classification of industrial properties.

MARKET TRENDS

The industrial property sector covers a broad, eclectic array of space users and property subtypes. The combinations and permutations of the demand/supply equation argue for a new, more precise classification of properties. To help explain the forces that have led to the current array of products, this foreword has examined the key evolutionary forces that have affected space users and producers. The book examines the classification system, presenting a cross-sectional look at the industrial property sector. It describes the primary and secondary classes that satisfy the criteria outlined earlier in terms of uniqueness, distinctiveness, meaningfulness, substantiality, and sustainability.

The industrial property classification system presented in this book is intended to endure over time, but the reality is that the dynamic nature of the market likely will necessitate adjustments. Because major structural shifts or revolutions such as technology and the new economy will occur, it is important to identify the major external and internal trends that will have an impact in the near term. Insight about emerging trends will be particularly

FOREWORD

helpful to the more proactive developers and investors who tend to operate on the edge and approach real estate in general, and industrial properties in particular, as short-term plays. With respect to industrial properties, two key types of trends are noteworthy: external trends that affect the broader business and economic environment, and internal trends that affect industrial space users, space producers, and market facilitators.

EXTERNAL TRENDS

Globalization, Consolidation, and Securitization. Three major external trends will likely continue to influence the evolution of the industrial market: globalization, consolidation, and securitization. Much has been written about them. For the purposes of this book, they are explored in general terms with an emphasis on how they might affect the future market for industrial space.

The globalization of businesses, economies, and finance affects industrial real estate both directly and indirectly. As a result, business forecasts and strategic plans must consider global economic conditions, and companies must operate on a more global, diverse plane. Similarly, the globalization of finance has tremendous implications on real estate capital flows, affecting the relative demand for investments and ultimately the cost of capital. Likewise, the growth of multinational companies domiciled in the United States and based offshore has created a network of businesses that transcend national boundaries and parochial concerns. As the global market matures, relative economic roles can be expected to emerge, with various countries and locations playing dominant roles in the areas in which they have a competitive advantage, thus changing demand for industrial space.

The consolidation of industry continues to unfold, penetrating deeper into industries and cutting across sectors and global boundaries. Like globalization, consolidation affects industrial needs both indirectly and directly. Although its effects are still being played out, the trend will clearly result in a greater concentration of power and an increased homogenization of services and responses to external conditions that indirectly affect the industrial market. The concentration of industrial activity in the hands of well-capitalized public and private entities, replacing smaller, generally local predecessors, will have a direct impact on both demand and supply.

The securitization of real estate markets also has affected materially the way the domestic real estate market operates. Because many investors will invest in both private and public structures, management philosophies are expected to converge, resulting in advances in best practices and more precise, sophisticated investment strategies and practices. With respect to industrial investments, which are becoming more diverse and complicated, investors will seek out players who are best capable of responding to the opportunities that emerge during this evolutionary process.

Technological Innovation. Unlike globalization, consolidation, and securitization, the technological revolution has led to a seemingly endless series of new paradigms and response paths. This situation reflects a dramatic departure from more gradual evolutionary change, which richly rewarded innovators and early adapters able to capitalize on new opportunities. Unfortunately, logical, disciplined approaches break down in the face of rapid technological changes, leaving businesses and real estate professionals alike to face a difficult dilemma: either adopt emerging technology trends as they unfold, or wait until some clear direction indicates where new trends are headed and what they mean to business processes. In the case of industrial real estate, such a passive, risk-averse approach could, on the one hand, expose developers and investors to a series of wipeouts by leaving them with functionally obsolescent facilities. On the other hand, by overreacting they could be left holding overimproved facilities for which companies would be unwilling or unable to pay the premium rent required to amortize the added expense. Since technological innovations are likely to continue to emerge, industrial investors and portfolio managers must develop financially feasible and sustainable response systems to such technological trends.

INTERNAL TRENDS

Supply Chain Management. The term *supply chain management* refers to the integration of procurement, production, pricing, logistics, and other business functions associated with providing goods and services. During the 1980s, interest in supply chains was focused largely on transportation issues as companies struggled with how to get their products to market in a more timely and cost-effective manner. In the early 1990s, the notion of supply chains was broadened to include the warehousing function, setting the stage for a more comprehensive approach to the field. As manufacturers began to appreciate the added value of more comprehensive supply chain systems, many of them turned to third-party logistics (3PL) providers to capture the benefits promised by applying more-sophisticated management tools. Over time, emphasis shifted from approaching supply chains as a cost-containment model to viewing them as tools that can create competitive advantage.

The contemporary approach to supply chain management is comprehensive, incorporating state-of-the-art advances in such subareas as planning and scheduling, distribution planning and deployment, inventory management, material handling systems, outbound/fulfillment, trading partners, transportation management, and warehouse management. While some firms have developed in-house capabilities for supply chain management, many have turned to outsourcing to capture the benefits without incurring the overhead and costs associated with in-house approaches. This trend has become even more pronounced as best practices have improved dramatically, creating windfalls for those who can stay on the cutting edge of innovation and wipeouts for those who lag behind and fail to remain competitive. In this environment, supply chains are becoming more interconnected, creating greater dependencies in which companies look to their suppliers and facilitators to help improve customer satisfaction and responsiveness and focus their efforts on their core capabilities.

Advances in two subareas of the supply chain—logistics and procurement—are particularly noteworthy to industrial real estate. Logistics—an important subset of the broader area of supply chain management—has undergone dramatic changes triggered by the e-business, Internet, and technological revolution. For example, changing logistical models associated with technological advances and elimination of middlemen in many industries have dramatically affected the level, design, and location of desired facilities. On a related note, the use of technology-enhanced inventory tracking and shipping systems, coupled with more efficient approaches to packaging and logistics management, has set the stage for further disintermediation of middleman. As a result, many companies now bypass the use of traditional storage facilities in favor of direct manufacturer-to-end-user shipping. On another front, changes in production, as companies increasingly look at improving productivity by reengineering manufacturing processes, have also changed manufacturing channels. Going forward, supply chain management will continue to be one of the more dynamic fields for industrial investors to monitor as a wave of new computer-tracking, communication, and distribution systems technologies are expected to emerge.

FOREWORD

Technology Integration. Technological innovation, as well as the successful integration of technology, has been one of the driving forces behind the advances that have been made in supply chain management and improved productivity levels in manufacturing. Although some might view these as new changes directly resulting from the Internet and e-business explosion, many of the technology-induced innovations actually have been on the scene for a number of years. Such innovations include automated warehousing, product tracking, production modeling, direct order processing, and improved fulfillment processes. Thus, for seasoned observers and those actively engaged in the industrial sector, many of the changes are more evolutionary than revolutionary. However, close attention must also be paid to unexpected technological innovations or other advances, such as increased use of automation, which have the potential to improve manufacturing productivity or materially change business processes.

In this increasingly dynamic industrial environment, innovation and successful integration of technology can clearly affect real estate demand, influencing both the site-selection process and design features required by tenants. Changes in business processes and compressed product life cycles will translate to a preference for more flexible leases. To stay on top of these trends and help quantify their effect on the broader industrial sector, attention should be paid to the more innovative space users. Advances in the shipping and logistics sectors—where locational preferences are shifting toward greater airport accessibility, shipments are tracked on a real-time basis, and hub-and-spoke distribution models have been developed to accommodate drop shipping—can also provide insights. Given the durable, capital-intensive nature of real estate, technological advances must be identified that will have a lasting effect on real estate use or market processes.

Changing distribution models for the retailing industry provide another example of evolving business functions and technological integration that are affecting warehouse demand. In the highly competitive retail arena, a number of retailers are developing highly refined and technologically dependent distribution systems. The heightened awareness of retailers to micromarket merchandise (i.e., customizing inventory to local demand) to satisfy an increasingly eclectic and dynamic consumer base also is causing changes in logistics management. These needs affect the physical design of warehouses in order to handle vertical distribution, the size of facilities to achieve necessary economies of scale, and the location of such facilities. In the area of facilitation, growth of the Internet and extranets supports the emergence of extended enterprises that foster greater interaction and collaboration. In addition to improving communication, such efforts can help improve throughput from businesses to consumers. For example, many stores are shifting to manufacturer-added electronic article surveillance (EAS) source tagging that adds surveillance labels on goods before their delivery to the store. Although there is no current industry standard for such tags, the competing technologies most likely will be reconciled, adding even more efficiency. Increasing use of computer-assisted logistics and scanner technology also makes it easier to manage distribution processes and respond to smaller order size to ensure that stores have adequate supplies without requiring large in-store storage spaces.

FOREWORD

CONCLUSION

The industrial property sector is a property class that meets the diverse needs of a wide range of users who in turn are undergoing dramatic changes in basic business processes and supply chains. The objective of this book is to capture, organize, and explain this diversity to help industrial real estate developers and investors develop more sophisticated approaches to this important component of the broader commercial real estate market. Rather than merely expand on the generally accepted typology, the book introduces a new structure that includes six primary categories and 12 secondary categories. Although the bulk of the book focuses on the physical characteristics of the various industrial building classes, it also provides insight into the nature of tenants that such facilities can best house in an efficient, cost-effective manner.

To provide additional understanding of the various components of the broader industrial sector, the book explores how the various classes fit in the overall supply chain and highlights some of the spatial and market commonalities within each of the categories. The standardization and precision provided by the proposed classification system should help advance professional practices, creating a more efficient system for balancing the spatial and capital market in terms of industrial property. At the same time, the classification should help developers approach the sector in a more strategic manner. It should also help investors select properties and financial arrangements that help them capture superior risk-adjusted returns from the industrial sector and, at a broader level, for an overall real estate portfolio. This book should help developers and investors develop a greater empathy with various segments of tenants, providing some insight into the driving forces behind the current demand for industrial space. Finally, the trends briefly introduced in this book should help developers and investors gauge future demand, suggesting what issues need to be monitored to manage industrial real estate activities in a more proactive manner to provide sustainable results that exploit market inefficiencies and capitalize on new opportunities.

James R. DeLisle
Director, Runstad Center for Real Estate Studies
University of Washington
Seattle, Washington

INTRODUCTION AND SUMMARY

INTRODUCTION

Constituting the largest sector of U.S. real estate, both in terms of square footage and of value, industrial real estate encompasses approximately 25 billion square feet of space. It includes manufacturing plants, warehouses, research and development (R&D) centers, air cargo facilities, and a number of other building types. Industrial real estate has a wide variety of sizes, shapes, and buildouts. Virtually every American business directly or indirectly relies on some form of industrial real estate to manufacture, warehouse, or distribute goods. This guide provides a look at the world of American industrial real estate. In addition to presenting a structure for the classification of industrial real estate, the guide analyzes the use, evolution, location, supply chain placement, and investment performance of each category.

CATEGORIES OF INDUSTRIAL REAL ESTATE

Notwithstanding the varied use and design of specific buildings, all types of industrial real estate have common characteristics. These common characteristics can be classified within six primary, and 12 secondary, categories. Certain types of industrial buildings—such as bulk warehouse facilities—have a recognized history of use; others—such as rack-supported buildings—are new to the sector. The accompanying table lists the six primary categories and 12 secondary categories of U.S. industrial real estate defined in this guide.

PRIMARY CATEGORIES	SECONDARY CATEGORIES
Warehouse distribution	Regional warehouse
	Bulk warehouse
	Heavy distribution
	Refrigerated distribution
	Rack-supported warehouse
Manufacturing	Light manufacturing
	Heavy manufacturing
	Airport hangar
Flex	R&D flex
	Office showroom
Multitenant	
Freight forwarding	Truck terminal
	Air cargo
Data switch center	

INTRODUCTION

Historically, industrial buildings have been classified according to a combination of physical characteristics and use in three primary categories: warehouse, manufacturing, and flex. These three categories encompassed approximately 90 percent of the total industrial stock, but major classification issues remained unresolved. Buildings with widely varying characteristics were included within the same broad categories and some buildings were misclassified because of a lack of definitive categories. Other buildings were ignored completely—more than 2 billion square feet of existing buildings were unclassified.

A new two-level system of classification introduced in this guide acknowledges the variations within the three historical categories of warehouse, manufacturing, and flex while also providing three new categories—freight forwarding, multitenant, and data switch center. Most important, this new system expands the coverage of industrial real estate to almost 100 percent of the national inventory, excluding only certain industrial buildings that do not fit in any of these categories because of their hybrid form.

CLASSIFICATION PROCESS

Industrial real estate may be classified according to its use or its physical characteristics. This guide uses the latter method of classification because it recognizes design features that may not be apparent with the use classification approach.

The process of classifying industrial real estate by physical characteristics uses core and ancillary differentiating features. *Core differentiating features* are those physical characteristics that are present in all buildings within the same category. For example, all truck terminals have docks on parallel walls, which is a core feature that differentiates this building type. *Ancillary differentiating features* are common, but not always present, within a particular industrial category. For example, trailer parking is common but not always present in heavy distribution buildings; therefore this feature is an ancillary characteristic differentiating heavy distribution buildings. Several industrial categories can have some of the same core or ancillary physical characteristics, or both. The presence of docks along at least two walls is a core differentiating characteristic of both truck terminals and heavy distribution buildings. However, truck terminals and heavy distribution buildings have other core characteristics that are not identical, so separate categories are required that recognize those differences.

INTRODUCTION

PHYSICAL BUILDING CHARACTERISTICS

The unique physical characteristics of industrial buildings distinguish them from other classes of real estate assets. The typical physical features of industrial real estate include multiple loading docks, deep truck courts, high ceilings, and the presence of cranes. The same attributes that distinguish industrial buildings from those of other real estate sectors also form the six distinct primary categories within this sector.

The historically used warehouse, manufacturing, and flex categories do not adequately encompass the diverse world of industrial real estate. Truck terminals, for example, were combined in a category with warehouse buildings, although the terminals generally do not warehouse goods, their ceilings are low, and they rarely have racking. Likewise, multitenant buildings do not fit within the three-category system and were included with both manufacturing and warehouse buildings. As another example, a recent surge in the creation of data and switch centers both by redevelopment of older buildings and through new construction has resulted in what is clearly a new category of industrial real estate. The range of physical differences for buildings within each primary category justifies the creation of secondary categories. The physical characteristics of warehouse distribution facilities, for example, vary significantly from building to building: ceiling heights range from 16 to 80 feet, the ratio of space per loading dock varies from 3,000 to 15,000 square feet, the amount of office space ranges from less than 5 percent to more than 25 percent.

Both interior and exterior features are used in classifying industrial real estate. Some building types can be classified by examining their exterior or interior features only. However, it is important to recognize that all secondary categories of industrial real estate have specific exterior and interior attributes. The principal exterior features are

- Building size
- Site coverage
- Loading capability
- Car and trailer parking.

The main interior features are

- Ceiling heights
- Space buildout
- Power
- Floor load and floor levelness.

Buildings can be classified correctly in the six primary and 12 secondary categories of industrial real estate by examining exterior and interior physical features and determining the correct ranges of values for those features. This guide presents the range of values for each industrial building type, as well as additional variables for facilities with unique physical characteristics.

INTRODUCTION

BUILDING USE

Industrial real estate has a diversity of use not found in other sectors of real estate. For example, office buildings can accommodate a variety of businesses classified under various industrial codes of the North American Industry Classification System (NAICS). However, the overall use of the space is relatively uniform. Industrial facilities accommodate not only a wide variety of businesses but also a wide range of activities, each of which requires a specific environment and physical structure. Manufacturing, testing, warehousing, and distributing activities directly correspond to four of the primary industrial real estate categories: manufacturing, flex, warehouse distribution, and freight forwarding. These industrial activities can be further specialized. Manufacturing, for example, includes processing raw materials, assembling products, and maintaining them. Those activities correspond to the secondary categories within manufacturing: heavy manufacturing, light manufacturing, and airport hangar.

A building's use is an important classification tool that can confirm a classification made on the basis of physical characteristics and, in some cases, serves as the final determinant. For example, whereas truck terminals are identified by their physical exterior appearance, light manufacturing buildings are identified by their activity, or use. Certain industrial real estate categories have flexible physical characteristics that can accommodate multiple activities. Although R&D flex facilities cannot be used to perform freight forwarding without total redevelopment, a manufacturing company can perform light manufacturing within a bulk warehouse. This facility, therefore, would be classified by its use (light manufacturing) rather than by its physical characteristics (bulk warehouse). When a building's physical flexibility of design permits multiple uses, building use is the final determinant of classification.

In summary, the classification of an industrial building type by use is as important a process as classification by physical characteristics. It is important, however, to thoroughly understand the physical characteristics of all six primary and 12 secondary categories of industrial real estate as described in this guide.

SUMMARY

WAREHOUSE DISTRIBUTION

The warehouse distribution category comprises the largest number of secondary categories of all primary industrial categories because of its diversity and large market share. The secondary categories—regional warehouse, bulk warehouse, heavy distribution, refrigerated distribution, and rack-supported warehouse—differ, yet they share certain common physical characteristics.

The warehouse distribution category derives from the two primary functions of warehousing and distribution, which require specific physical characteristics. Most warehouse distribution buildings are rectangular in shape, which is conducive to efficient warehousing and distribution. Ceiling heights range from 16 to nearly 80 feet. Warehouse distribution facilities have loading requirements that exceed those of all other industrial categories except freight forwarding, requiring from 3,000 to 15,000 square feet per loading dock. The average for the category is 10,000 square feet per dock, with a higher ratio in buildings that warehouse only, reaching up to 15,000 square feet per dock.

Generally, warehouse distribution facilities have similar patterns of evolution across U.S. markets; however, that similarity does not apply to all secondary categories. The three most numerous secondary categories—regional warehouse, bulk warehouse, and heavy distribution—have common evolutionary patterns. The location of these facilities follows the population expansion of metropolitan areas: older buildings are located in the metropolitan center; newer buildings are located farther from the center. The average age of warehouse distribution facilities, therefore, decreases proportionately to their distance from the metropolitan center. Refrigerated distribution and rack-supported buildings do not follow this evolutionary pattern. The industrial category of refrigerated distribution is not expanding. The rack-supported category is too scarce in the United States to demonstrate a definitive pattern of evolution.

Buildings in the warehouse distribution category respond to the same four primary variables—two demographic and two infrastructure—with respect to location. Because the cost of land is high in higher-income areas, warehouse distribution facilities are located in lower-average-household-income areas. Such buildings also cluster in areas with a higher blue-collar workforce, although this relationship is less pronounced than it is with manufacturing facilities, which generally employ more workers per square foot than warehouse distribution buildings. With regard to infrastructure, warehousing and distribution require easy accessibility; therefore warehouse distribution facilities are located predominantly along highways and major roads. These buildings also tend to cluster around airports because of lower land prices, easy accessibility, and availability of airfreight services.

In combination with demographic and infrastructure variables, zoning affects the specific location of warehouse distribution buildings. These buildings generate heavy truck traffic, which is undesirable and thus discouraged in many areas. The location of warehouse distribution facilities, however, is not as restricted as that of manufacturing facilities.

Warehouse distribution facilities constitute approximately 14 billion square feet of U.S. industrial space. The necessary investment in land, construction, tenant improvements, and commissions for these facilities is lower overall than for flex and manufacturing buildings. Although this lower level of investment reduces risk, it generates slightly lower investment returns than the more risky industrial categories such as flex.

SUMMARY

MANUFACTURING

Manufacturing is the second-largest class of industrial property. The process of manufacturing is more diverse than that of warehousing or distribution and there are an almost infinite number of manufacturing, assembly, and repair-related processes. Each process requires specific building features and configurations. Classifying manufacturing facilities in the secondary categories of light manufacturing, heavy manufacturing, and airport hangar captures this diversity.

Because of their diversity, only two core differentiating features apply to manufacturing facilities: a high percentage of manufacturing space buildout and a high power requirement. The interior of a manufacturing building consists of warehouse and office space but emphasizes manufacturing space. The minimum manufacturing, assembly, and repair space required is 50 percent; the average is approximately 70 percent. The influence of heavy manufacturing facilities, which dedicate more than 90 percent of their space to manufacturing, accounts for this high average. The heavy power requirement of these facilities relates to the manufacturing process, which typically involves heavy machinery that, in turn, requires heavy power. Certain data switch centers have higher power requirements; however, because all secondary categories of manufacturing require heavy power, that is a core feature differentiating the category.

Manufacturing facilities have a number of ancillary differentiating features. Exterior features include minimal loading, rail service, and a high ratio of parking per square foot. Interior features include heavy floor loads and the presence of cranes.

There are differences in the expansionary evolutionary patterns for the secondary categories of buildings in the manufacturing primary category. Because the location of manufacturing buildings always depends on zoning, and frequently on rail service, they tend to be clustered. Both old and new buildings occupy the same area once it is zoned for industrial use. Airport hangars have no expansionary evolutionary pattern because they are confined to airports.

Zoning is the primary factor affecting the location of manufacturing buildings. Because manufacturing facilities accommodate labor-intensive processes, these facilities concentrate in areas where there are blue-collar workers. Whereas a metropolitan market's white-collar population typically moves outward from the center, the blue-collar population remains more stationary. Average household income is another demographic variable correlated with manufacturing, and these types of facilities are not present in the highest-income areas of geographic markets. Beyond zoning, location responds to the cost of land, environmental restrictions, and the general physical appearance of these buildings.

Manufacturing buildings are often owner-occupied, which results in a lack of available income and investment data for the category. National and local real estate market data are available, however, which indicate that the manufacturing category is a stable property type with lower-than-average vacancy rates. The market share of manufacturing facilities in the United States has been declining, a significant trend that is expected to continue.

SUMMARY

FLEX

The third-largest and most extensively tracked industrial category, flex is also the most difficult to categorize. Flex facilities have pronounced characteristics that differentiate the category from other primary categories, but these characteristics are too subtle to further classify flex facilities into clear secondary categories. Therefore, this diverse category has two secondary categories only: research and development (R&D) flex and office showroom, which differ significantly.

This category is known for the flexibility of its buildings' space configurations, which is a core differentiating feature. Two buildings that are identical from the exterior can have entirely different interior buildouts. The types of space commonly found in flex facilities are office, high-tech manufacturing, clean space/laboratory, and warehouse. The variety and proportion of configurations for these spaces are too numerous to create different secondary types for each.

A core feature differentiating flex facilities is their high percentage of office space, which ranges from 25 to 80 percent, exceeding that of all other industrial categories. High curb appeal, or an attractive exterior appearance, is another core feature of flex facilities. Office buildout, use of upscale construction materials, and officelike atmosphere and landscaping make flex buildings resemble single-story office buildings. As a result, flex facilities create a bridge between the industrial and office real estate sectors.

The presence of retail space is an additional characteristic associated with flex facilities, specifically office showrooms. Retail space can account for as much as 20 percent of a building.

R&D flex facilities and office showrooms exist in clusters of both new and old structures. Most large industrial markets have an area or submarket that is dominated by flex facilities.

Different demographic variables affect the location of R&D flex facilities and office showrooms. The resemblance of R&D flex facilities to office buildings influences their location; like office buildings, they are located in higher-income areas. The obstacles that exclude other industrial building types from higher-income areas—high cost of land, and zoning and environmental restrictions—do not apply as readily to R&D flex buildings because of their appearance, rents, and tenant base. Because of their retail component, office showrooms correlate more to the variable of total retail spending than to average house-hold income.

Investment and income data are readily available for the flex category. Overall investment per square foot in flex facilities is high across the components of land, construction, tenant improvements, and commissions. This higher investment results in higher rents. Flex facilities command the second-highest rents of all industrial facilities, following only data switch centers. Flex buildings generate a higher rate of return on investment, which is a function of the higher risk associated with their ownership. The higher risk is a function of lower-credit tenants and the increased cost of re-leasing a vacated building.

SUMMARY

MULTITENANT

Although strong core differentiating features distinguish multitenant from other industrial facilities, differences among multitenant buildings are too subtle to create secondary categories. Three core differentiating features unite all multitenant facilities: building size, design, and multitenant buildout. All multitenant facilities are smaller in size, generally not exceeding 120,000 square feet. The buildings are nonrectangular in design, most commonly configured in *L* and *U* shapes. They have multiple tenants. The size and design of a multitenant facility efficiently accommodate multiple tenant use, and the nonrectangular shape and smaller dimensions of the buildings limit efficient use by a single tenant. Most individual tenant spaces range from 5,000 to 15,000 square feet.

Multitenant facilities have versatile space buildout that can accommodate a variety of businesses. Space use differs from building to building, and from tenant unit to tenant unit. For example, a single multitenant building can efficiently accommodate a small manufacturer, a distributor, and a retailer.

Because of their small size and versatility, multitenant buildings have a random evolution and location pattern. Buildings of all ages are located both close to the metropolitan center and farther away. Clustering is minimal. Like all other industrial categories, multitenant buildings are subject to zoning restrictions.

Although access to blue-collar labor is commonly associated with industrial real estate, there is not a strong relationship between the location of multitenant facilities and this population demographic because of their small size and broad dispersion. However, multitenant buildings are generally located in lower-income areas. Consistent with the industrial sector, only a small percentage of the facilities are located in higher-income areas, and there are no facilities in the highest-income areas. Access to highways is less important for multitenant buildings than for warehouse distribution and freight-forwarding facilities.

Because multitenant buildings historically were not classified as a separate industrial category, historical investment and market data do not exist. However, within the largest U.S. markets multitenant buildings have slightly higher than average asking rents. Their availability is below the all-type average. Overall investment required in multitenant buildings is midrange between the warehouse distribution and flex categories. Because the necessary investment is sufficiently high, the buildings are not viewed as commodities.

SUMMARY

FREIGHT FORWARDING

Four types of transportation—road, rail, water, and air—are used to forward freight, which usually takes place without the use of a building. Only two freight-forwarding processes consistently use physical structures: intramodal, which involves trucks to trucks, and intermodal, which largely involves airplanes and trucks. The buildings that use these two distinct processes have sufficiently different physical characteristics to classify them in two secondary categories—truck terminal and air cargo.

The process of freight forwarding imposes on these facilities specific physical requirements that become the buildings' core physical characteristics. Freight-forwarding buildings have strict loading requirements. The buildings are cross-docked with a low ratio of square footage to docks. The ideal ratio for truck terminals is 500 square feet per dock. The distance for the movement of freight from one wall of docks to the opposite wall is ideally minimized. Thus, the buildings are rectangular in shape and always longer than they are deep to facilitate freight forwarding. A width of approximately 60 feet is considered ideal; there is no preferred length. Site coverage is low, around 20 percent, due to deep truck courts and truck trailer parking requirements, which ideally equal one space per dock. Interior space buildout for freight forwarding facilities differs significantly from other industrial categories. The sole purpose of freight-forwarding facilities is to move goods through, not to warehouse or manufacture. Office and warehouse space is, therefore, minimal. Manufacturing space is absent. Most space in these facilities is dedicated to sorting.

The freight-forwarding category has no defined evolutionary pattern. Air cargo facilities are limited to airport locations, which eliminates geographical expansion. Truck terminals have a number of restrictions and requirements, including zoning and access to highways.

Zoning and access to highway infrastructure primarily determine the location of freight-forwarding buildings. Of those demographic variables that affect the location of industrial buildings, only average household income exhibits a relationship with freight-forwarding facilities, specifically truck terminals. Truck terminals are located in lower-income areas, a consistent demographic characteristic of the overall industrial sector. Because of air cargo's specific location constraints, those facilities do not have any additional location drivers.

Freight-forwarding facilities historically have been classified in the warehouse distribution category, resulting in the unavailability of investment and market data. However, typical tenants of truck terminals are trucking companies, which generally have lower credit. Therefore, truck terminals are considered riskier investments and require higher capitalization rates than other major industrial building types. Also, both truck terminals and air cargo facilities are highly specialized, which complicates the process of re-leasing them, adding to the risk and justifying a higher required return on investment. Higher returns are achieved through relatively high rents, which are justified by the scarcity of older truck terminals and constraints on new construction due to zoning regulations.

SUMMARY

DATA SWITCH CENTER

The data switch center is the newest primary industrial category. It encompasses two seemingly different facility types: a data warehouse and a switch center. Since the only physical difference between the two is a power requirement (data warehouses have a higher power need), both can be combined within one category.

These types of telecommunications facilities can be developed by converting an older building that has access to fiber optic cable or by constructing a new building solely for telecommunications use. Both converted and newly constructed buildings have the same physical requirements. Access to heavy power is essential for data switch centers and is, therefore, a core physical characteristic. The power requirement ranges from 60 to 200 watts per square foot within these facilities. High floor load capacity is necessary to support the heavy telecommunications equipment, such as switches. System redundancy, or backup, is needed for heating, ventilating, and air conditioning (HVAC); security; and fire suppression. Increased security, raised floors, and gas-based fire-suppression systems with early detection are additional physical characteristics.

Most data switch centers were constructed in the late 1990s, making the category too new to have an established evolutionary pattern. Because these facilities must have access to fiber optic cable in order to function, the developing evolutionary pattern for this category will correlate with expansion of fiber optic cable.

No other demographic- or infrastructure-related variables seriously affect the location of data switch centers. These facilities employ the lowest number of workers of all industrial categories. Therefore, they do not require proximity to a labor pool. The buildings have an attractive exterior, especially the newer ones, and do not generate truck traffic. Unlike most industrial buildings, data switch centers can exist in higher-income areas. Most data switch centers in dense urban areas are located in multistory buildings.

The telecommunications industry is too new to have generated historical investment and market data for data switch centers. Because the industry is new, it is also risky, with an inefficient market. In 1999 and 2000, the market favored owners, but by 2001 that was no longer the case. These inefficiencies should subside over time, but the current high investment and associated higher risk will persist, resulting in higher required returns on investment. Because the design, size, and configuration of these buildings are heavily influenced by technological advances, this property type is expected to undergo the most changes in the future.

INDUSTRIAL CLASSIFICATIONS

WAREHOUSE DISTRIBUTION

Warehouse distribution facilities constitute more than 55 percent of the entire national inventory of industrial real estate: approximately 14 billion square feet within the United States. As the largest industrial real estate category, warehouses go by a variety of descriptive names, including bulk warehouse, regional warehouse, office warehouse, and big-box warehouse. Each type of warehouse has a specific use, and each name describes a feature that is unique to that building type. *Bulk* and *big-box warehouses* refer to the size of the building. *Office warehouse* refers to the contents of the warehouse—a higher percentage of which is offices. All warehouses have common attributes that classify them within the primary category of warehouse distribution. In addition, specific warehouses share unique characteristics that separate them further into secondary categories.

The warehouse distribution category encompasses the functions of warehousing and distributing goods. The proportion of warehousing versus distribution varies according to building type. This variety of function within a category is an excellent example of the diversity of industrial real estate.

The core differentiating features of warehouses are overall building design, ceiling height, and loading capabilities. Most warehouse distribution buildings are rectangular, thus the use of the term "box" in some descriptions. In order to be classified as a warehouse, buildings must have exterior walls that allow efficient warehousing and distribution by a single tenant. Most buildings not meeting this requirement are classified as multitenant facilities. This exterior wall requirement does not mean that all warehouses *are* occupied by one tenant but, rather, that these buildings *could be* occupied by a single tenant.

Ceiling height is another core differentiating feature of warehouse distribution facilities. Ceiling heights range from a minimum of 16 feet to as high as 80 feet in certain rack-supported buildings.

Warehouse distribution facilities have loading requirements that exceed those of all other primary categories except freight forwarding. Warehousing and distribution involve moving goods at high volume and/or high frequency, which requires adequate loading capabilities. Warehouse distribution facilities accommodate from 3,000 to 15,000 square feet per dock, with the average facility containing approximately 10,000 square feet per dock.

Warehouse distribution comprises five secondary categories: regional warehouse, bulk warehouse, heavy distribution, refrigerated distribution, and rack-supported warehouse. The core features of the warehouse distribution category—building design, ceiling height, and loading capabilities—also apply to buildings in each of the secondary categories. Additional attributes unique to each secondary category include dock configuration, trailer parking, power resources, and floor load and levelness. These features are consistently present and recognizable in each secondary category.

WAREHOUSE DISTRIBUTION

	SIZE (SQUARE FEET)	PERCENTAGE OFFICE	PERCENTAGE MANUFACTURING	CEILING HEIGHT	DOCK RATIO	PERCENTAGE COOLER/ FREEZER
REGIONAL WAREHOUSE Regional warehouses are rectangular in shape, allowing more efficient single-tenant use. They generally do not exceed 100,000 square feet. Ceiling heights are at the low end of the warehouse distribution range. The primary function of these facilities is to store and distribute goods, serving the surrounding region.	Up to 100,000	Up to 25%	Up to 10%	16'–24'	1: 5,000–15,000	Up to 5%
BULK WAREHOUSE Bulk warehouses store large amounts of goods for varying lengths of time, ranging from extensive storage to almost immediate distribution. The building's use, combined with its size, determines the interior space buildout that is allocated to manufacturing, office, and warehouse.	Over 100,000	Up to 10%	Up to 10%	20' +	1: 5,000–10,000	Up to 5%
HEAVY DISTRIBUTION The design of heavy distribution buildings is conducive to the function of distribution, rather than warehousing. Heavy distribution buildings have docks along a minimum of two walls, perpendicular or parallel to each other. Site coverage is low because of truck maneuvering areas and trailer parking requirements.	Over 100,000	Below 5%	0%	24' +	Below 1: 5,000	None
REFRIGERATED DISTRIBUTION Although freezers and wheel-in coolers are common in other industrial building types, an incorporated freezer floor is an integral design feature in refrigerated distribution buildings. Because of this unique floor, it is not economical to convert refrigerated distribution buildings to other types of warehouse distribution facilities.	Any	Up to 15%	Some food processing	20'–30' +	1: 7,000–10,000	Over 25%
RACK-SUPPORTED WAREHOUSE In rack-supported buildings, racking provides both the structural support and storage space. A typical facility has separate storage and shipping areas. The shipping area resembles a standard warehouse with a number of docks and lower ceiling heights. The storage and shipping areas are typically connected by an automated conveyor system.	Any	Below 5%	0%	Can be over 60'	In the shipping area—1:5,000	None

WAREHOUSE DISTRIBUTION

REGIONAL WAREHOUSE

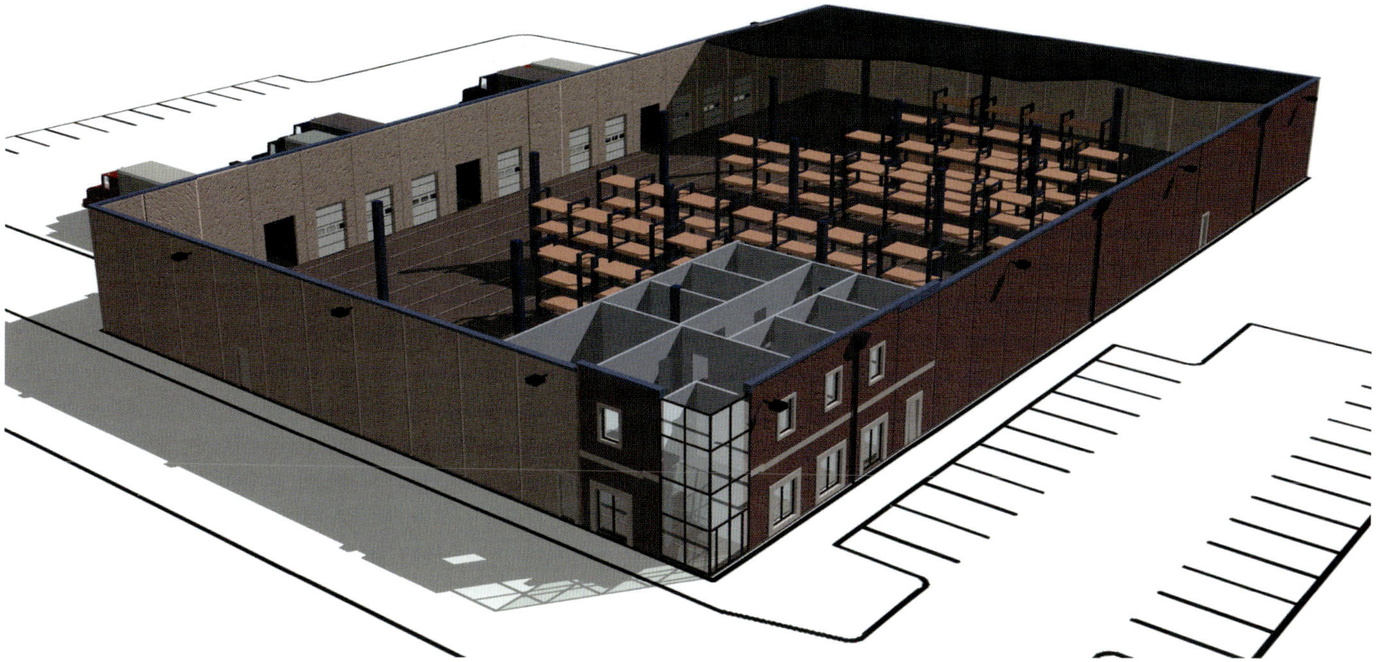

As a group, regional warehouses make up the largest number of facilities in the warehouse distribution category. They serve local and regional markets for storing and distributing goods.

Regional warehouses generally do not exceed 100,000 square feet in size. In cases where they are smaller, they may be referred to colloquially as "local" warehouses. They are similar in size to multitenant facilities but the shape of the two types of facilities distinguishes them from each other.

Regional warehouses are generally rectangular in shape and built for single tenants, although they can be adapted to multiple-tenant use. The amount of office buildout varies significantly. Regional warehouses may be called office warehouses in cases where there is a higher-than-usual percentage of office space.

Typically, little or no manufacturing activities take place within regional warehouses; therefore, they do not have the specific features required by manufacturers. When present, manufacturing space in regional warehouses rarely exceeds 10 percent of the total building size.

WAREHOUSE DISTRIBUTION

REGIONAL WAREHOUSE/ EXTERIOR

Regional warehouses are the smallest buildings in the warehouse distribution category. Their size, less than 100,000 square feet, differentiates them from bulk warehouses. The loading requirement of regional warehouses typically ranges from 5,000 to 15,000 square feet of interior space to one dock; the average is approximately 10,000 square feet per dock. The ratio varies, depending on the facility's use and number of tenants. Regional warehouses with multiple tenants and a high product turnover have a lower ratio: approximately 5,000 square feet to the one dock. Single-tenant buildings with a low product turnover have a higher ratio: approximately 15,000 square feet per dock. These loading requirements exceed those of manufacturing and flex facilities but not those of other distribution-oriented building types such as bulk warehouse, heavy distribution, and freight forwarding.

A land-to-building site coverage ratio of two to one is usual. Building coverage on the site corresponds to the level of office buildout and the resulting surface parking requirements.

WAREHOUSE DISTRIBUTION

REGIONAL WAREHOUSE/ INTERIOR

The interior of regional warehouses varies significantly depending upon the use and number of tenants. Single-tenant use is typical of regional warehouses. In cases where buildings are divided for use by multiple tenants, they may resemble multitenant buildings but there are distinctive differences. Their uniform, rectangular shape contrasts with that of multitenant buildings, which can be configured in irregular and narrow shapes with separate entrances serving individual tenants. Average tenant space in regional warehouses exceeds 20,000 square feet, which is approximately twice the average tenant space within multitenant buildings.

Regional warehouse facilities have the most varied tenant use in the warehouse distribution category. Some are designed to warehouse and others are used as distribution facilities. Office buildout generally ranges from 5 to 25 percent of total building size, depending on the number and size of tenants. Multitenant warehouses have a higher range of office buildout than single-tenant facilities. Dock accessibility varies among the buildings as well; both private and common docks are used.

Ceiling heights are typically lower than in most other warehouse distribution buildings, ranging from 16 to 24 feet. The lower ceiling height tends to preclude the buildout of mezzanine space for office use within the building.

WAREHOUSE DISTRIBUTION

REGIONAL WAREHOUSE/ EVOLUTION

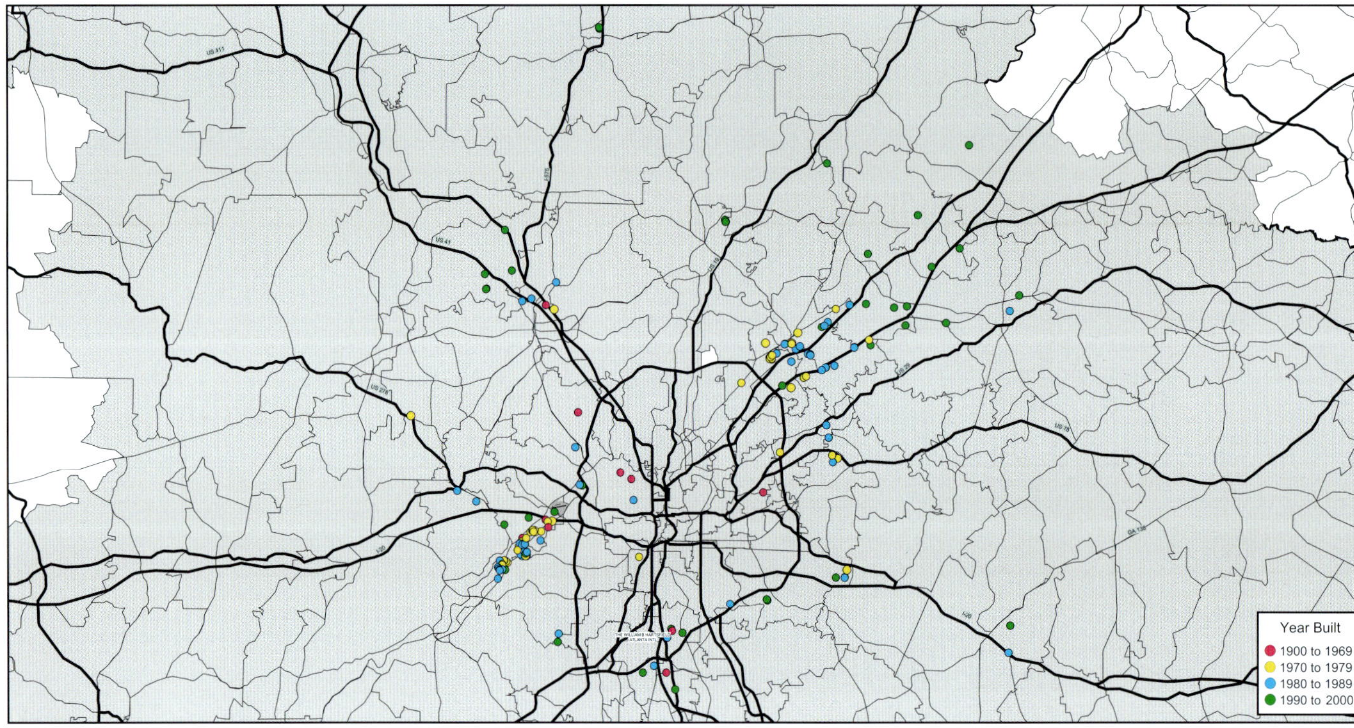

Atlanta.

Regional warehouse facilities serve a wide variety of tenants involved in warehousing and distributing goods. Tenants range from small, local distributors to large manufacturing corporations. Most space in these buildings is dedicated to storage and distribution. Interior buildout, however, can be allocated to light manufacturing space, which is ideal for small assemblers.

The accompanying map depicts 174 regional warehouses in the Atlanta metropolitan market. The evolutionary pattern of the warehouses follows population expansion. Older buildings, indicated by purple dots, are located within the center of the metropolitan area. Newer facilities, indicated by green dots, are located in areas farther out from the metropolitan center. Some newer facilities also are located closer to the metropolitan center, replacing older, obsolete buildings. This evolutionary pattern is representative of the warehouse distribution primary category overall. In spite of some overlap of older and newer buildings, which is a result of local area growth, regional warehouses in general follow population growth.

WAREHOUSE DISTRIBUTION

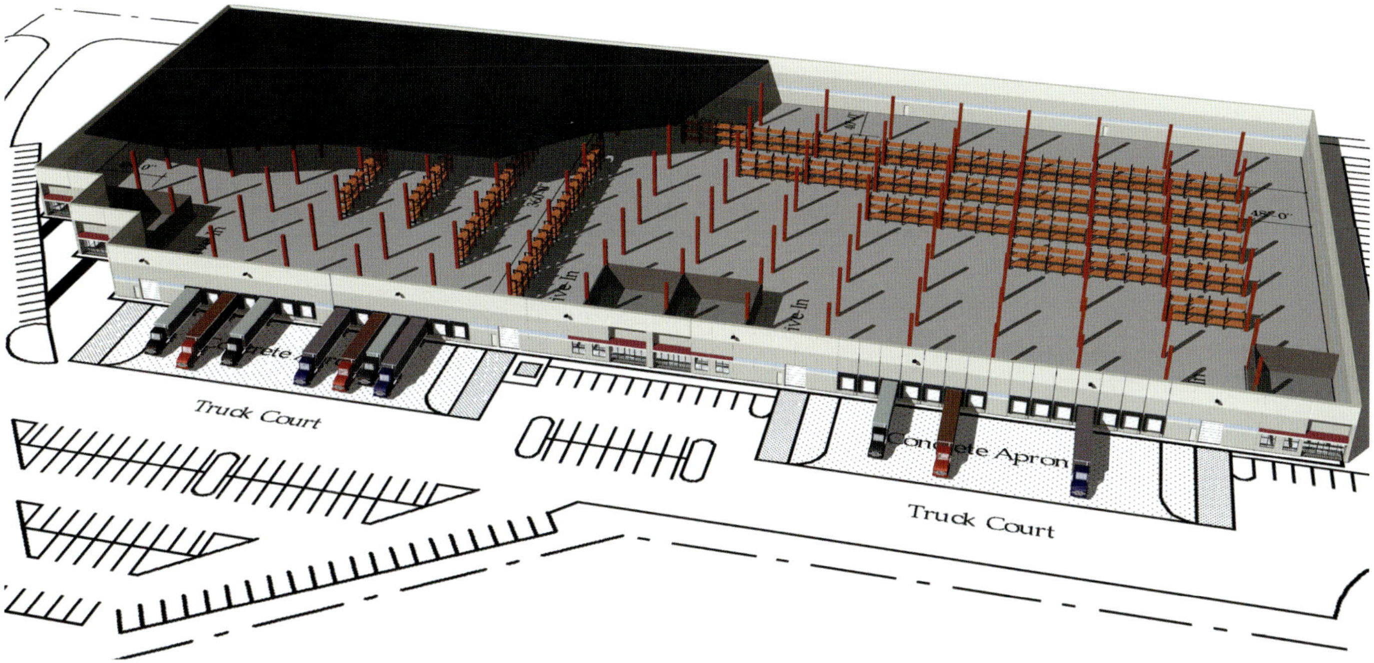

BULK WAREHOUSE

Bulk warehouses store large quantities of goods for varying periods of time, ranging from long-term storage to almost immediate distribution. Large in size—exceeding 100,000 square feet—these facilities are easy to identify. A building's overall use, combined with its size, determines the interior space that is allocated to warehouse, office, and manufacturing use. Bulk warehouses are generally not suitable for manufacturing because of their insufficient power resources, high ceilings, and large number of docks. When present, manufacturing space rarely exceeds 10 percent of the building area. Space allocated to offices is usually minimal.

In addition to size, other core features of bulk warehouse facilities are their extensive loading capabilities and high ceilings. Most loading and unloading activities are performed with the use of docks and, to a lesser extent, drive-in doors. Ceiling heights in bulk warehouses generally exceed 20 feet, with slightly lower ceilings in some older buildings. In newer buildings, advances in technology are pushing ceiling heights above 30 feet.

WAREHOUSE DISTRIBUTION

BULK WAREHOUSE/ EXTERIOR

Bulk warehouses are distinctive from the exterior because of their large size. With a minimum size of 100,000 square feet and a maximum size exceeding 1 million square feet, they are comparable in size to buildings in the manufacturing category. Site coverage, which is a function of parking, truck maneuvering areas, and trailer parking, is a feature that differentiates warehouses from manufacturing buildings. Because bulk warehouses do not employ as many individuals per square foot as most other warehouse distribution facilities, they require less automobile parking space, resulting in lower site coverage. However, they do require deep truck courts and trailer parking. On average, the typical site coverage ratio ranges up to 50 percent for bulk warehouses compared with approximately 40 percent for manufacturing facilities.

The quantity of goods flowing through bulk warehouses and the mode of transporting them are factors that differentiate bulk warehouses from other facilities. Truck service predominates; today, rail service is viewed within the industry as an amenity rather than as a necessity and is used primarily by industries that can ship and receive bulk goods competitively by rail. Ultimately, market practice in the treatment of the supply chain process determines the loading configuration incorporated into new buildings. The ratio commonly ranges from 5,000 to 10,000 square feet of space to one dock, with most bulk warehouse facilities having 10,000 square feet or less per dock. Certain bulk warehouses have both rail doors and truck docks for intermodal freight forwarding—that is, shifting goods from one type of transportation to another type (e.g., truck to train). However, intermodal transportation usually takes place at designated areas and is performed externally, without physical structures.

WAREHOUSE DISTRIBUTION

BULK WAREHOUSE/ INTERIOR

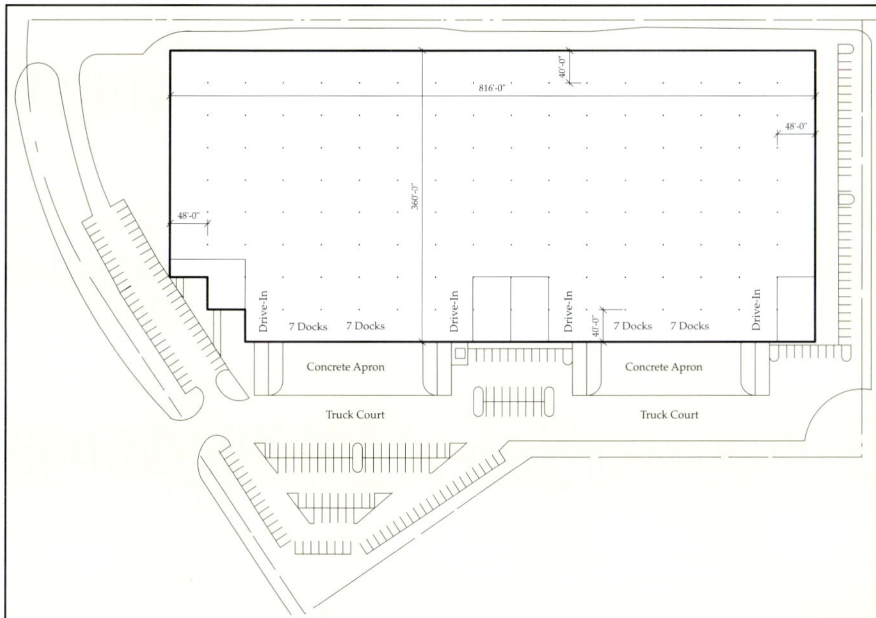

Ninety percent of bulk warehouse space is allocated to storage for large quantities of goods. The amount of space allocated to office use is minimal and typically is less than 10 percent of the building's overall size. In very large buildings, the office allocation may be closer to 5 percent and in certain smaller bulk warehouses office space may exceed 10 percent of the entire building. Manufacturing space also may be present in bulk warehouses; however, like the warehouse distribution category as a whole, bulk warehouses lack the attributes required by most manufacturing operations. Therefore, manufacturing space in bulk warehouses rarely exceeds 10 percent of the total building size and does not require a separate buildout.

The ceiling heights in bulk warehouses—20 to 30-plus feet in newer buildings—allow the insertion of a mezzanine floor while maintaining a consistent height throughout the entire structure. Bulk warehouses generally utilize racking systems, which require leveled and thick floors to bear heavy loads and minimize truck and train vibration. The volume of goods stored determines how thick the floor must be. Heavier goods, or a large quantity of goods, require a thicker floor. The minimum floor thickness is six inches, which allows for 4,000 pounds per square inch (PSI). The importance of floor thickness and levelness differentiates bulk warehouses from other industrial real estate categories.

WAREHOUSE DISTRIBUTION

BULK WAREHOUSE/ EVOLUTION

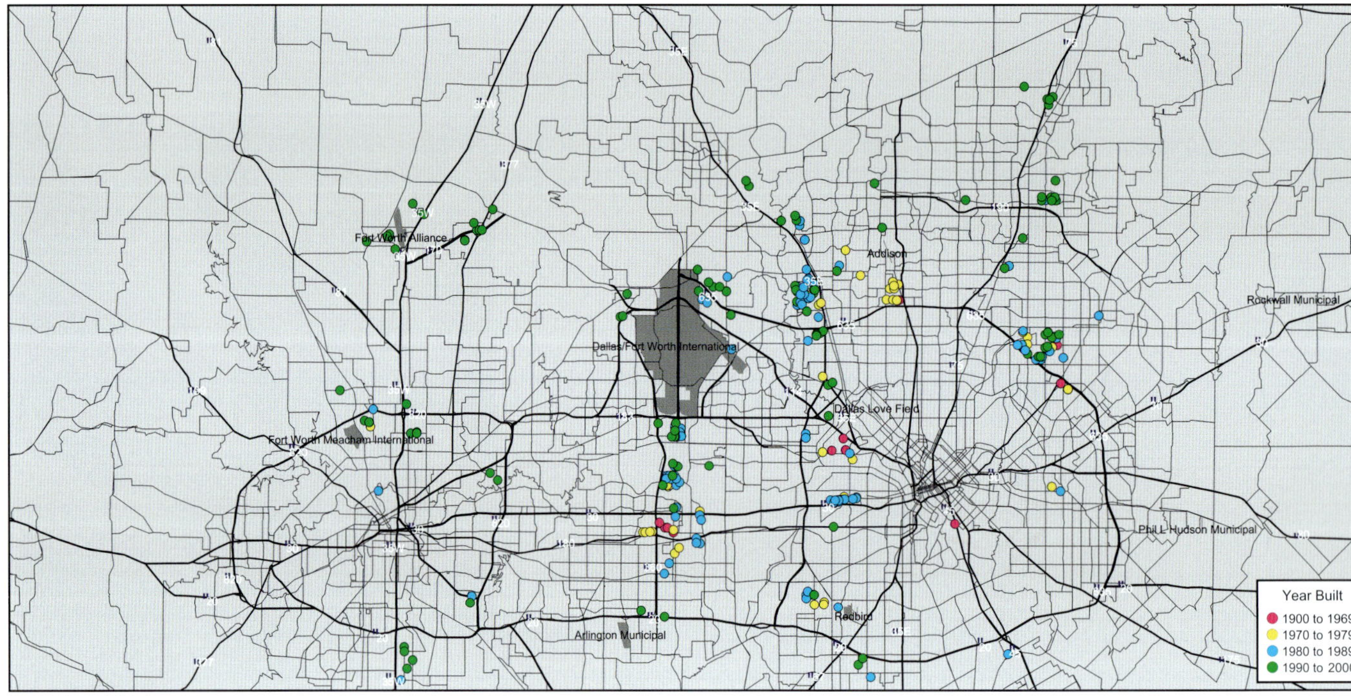

Dallas/Fort Worth.

Of all industrial building types, bulk warehouses have the widest variety of tenants. They range from manufacturing companies that store parts and goods to logistics companies that distribute goods for other companies and retailers that store products before shipping them to retail outlets or directly to consumers.

Bulk warehouses are larger and their ceilings are higher today than in the past. The sample displayed on the accompanying map of Dallas/ Fort Worth depicts 129 bulk warehouse buildings built in the 1990s, compared with 110 constructed in the 1980s. The difference in average building size between these two periods is 20,000 square feet per building, or approximately 10 percent.

The same sample demonstrates the average ceiling height for bulk warehouses has increased over the last 20 years from 23 feet, for those buildings constructed before 1980; to 25 feet, for buildings built during the 1980s; to 27.5 feet, for those built in the 1990s. New technology is the driving force behind these changes. Automated retrieval systems and inventory software used in modern warehouses allow more efficient storage of goods due to higher stacking capabilities.

Bulk warehouses follow a clear pattern of geographic expansion that is consistent with urban growth patterns. The accompanying map of Dallas/ Fort Worth clearly illustrates this pattern. Newer buildings—those constructed within the last 20 years—are located farthest from the city's center. Older buildings are situated closer to the metropolitan center. This pattern also can be found in Atlanta, Chicago, Los Angeles, and other major metropolitan areas.

WAREHOUSE DISTRIBUTION

HEAVY DISTRIBUTION

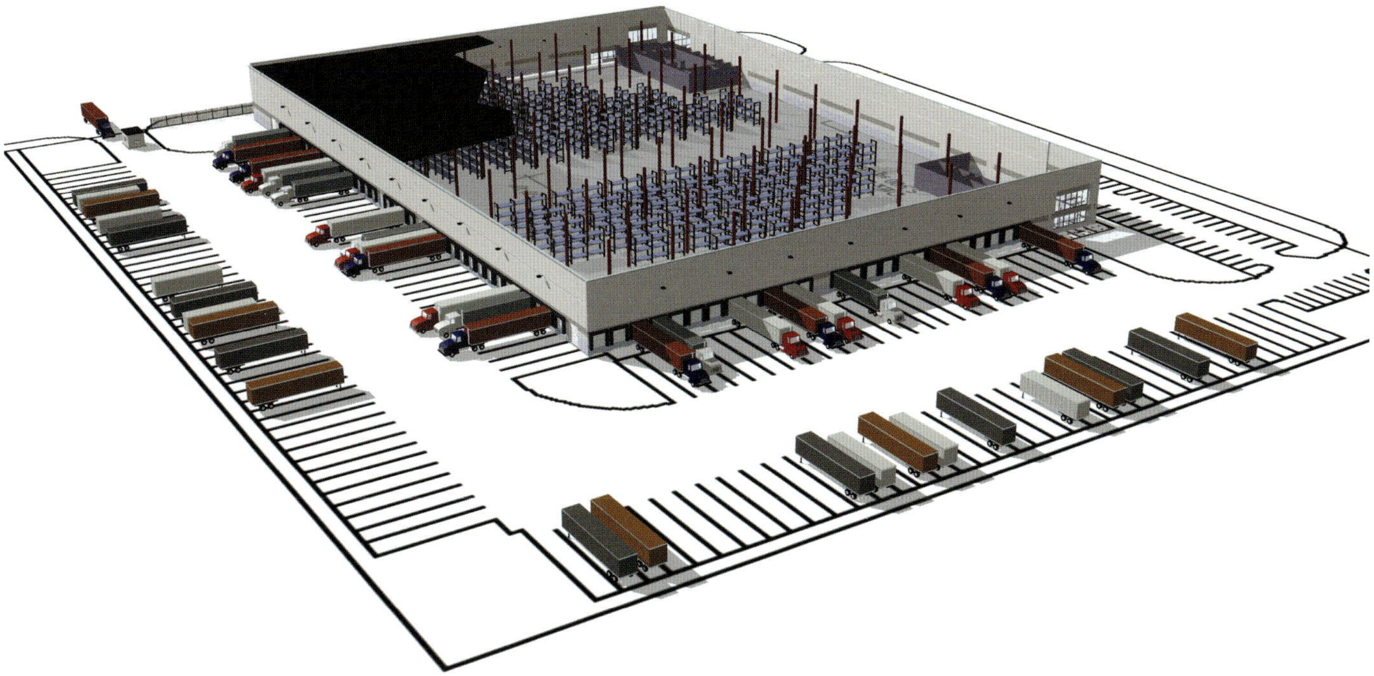

The design of heavy distribution buildings is geared toward accommodating distribution rather than warehousing. Nevertheless, heavy distribution buildings can warehouse goods for extended periods and, therefore, are similar to bulk warehouses, with which they share certain characteristics. The presence of loading docks along more than one wall is a core differentiating feature of heavy distribution facilities.

Large in size, heavy distribution buildings typically range from 100,000 to 500,000 square feet. Examples outside this size range exist but are rare. Ceilings in excess of 24 feet in height, and averaging 28 feet, are required for the warehousing function. The number of loading docks and their design differentiate heavy distribution from bulk warehouse facilities: bulk warehouses have a typical ratio of 10,000 square feet for one dock, whereas heavy distribution buildings have a ratio of less than 5,000 square feet for one dock.

WAREHOUSE DISTRIBUTION

HEAVY DISTRIBUTION/ EXTERIOR

Heavy distribution buildings can be distinguished by their dock configurations. Other warehouse distribution buildings usually have docks situated along only one wall; heavy distribution buildings must have docks along a minimum of two walls. Although by definition a cross-dock facility has docks on two parallel walls, heavy distribution facilities can have docks that are either perpendicular or parallel to each other. In most warehouse distribution buildings, the ratio of square feet per dock is approximately 3,500 square feet per dock. Because there are docks along more than one wall, the number of docks is higher and the ratio of square feet per dock is lower. Within the industrial real estate sector as a whole, heavy distribution buildings have the third-lowest ratio of square feet to docks, following those of truck terminals and air cargo buildings.

Building size and site coverage are clear identifying features of heavy distribution facilities. Buildings are a minimum of 100,000 square feet, similar to bulk warehouses. Smaller heavy distribution facilities do exist, however, especially in smaller markets. The average site coverage of heavy distribution buildings is approximately 30 to 40 percent, the lowest average coverage of all warehouse distribution facilities, because their distribution function and docking system require a larger perimeter for truck courts around the building. Trailer parking commonly is located on the site, which also significantly reduces site coverage.

WAREHOUSE DISTRIBUTION

HEAVY DISTRIBUTION/ INTERIOR

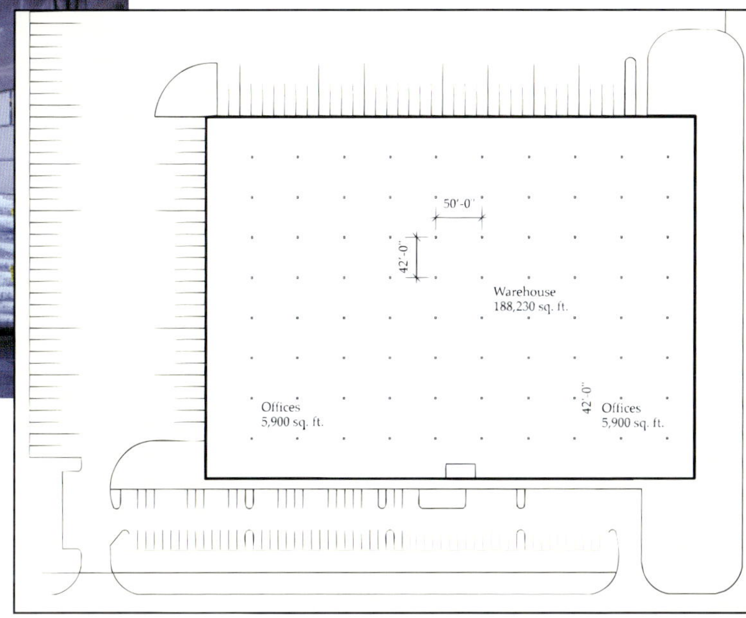

Even though the interiors of heavy distribution buildings resemble those of bulk warehouses, the former have certain unique physical characteristics. They rarely include more than 5 percent office space, and they have no manufacturing space. Buildings have a minimum ceiling height of 24 feet, and in most buildings, ceilings reach or exceed heights of 30 feet. Building depth—the maximum distance goods travel between place of storage and the closest dock for loading—is minimized in this building type since the emphasis is on distribution rather than warehousing. Heavy distribution buildings use both level floors, for racking, and thick floors, for supporting weight, which differentiates them from all other industrial real estate categories except bulk and rack-supported warehouses. Like those of bulk warehouses, the floor thickness and levelness of heavy distribution buildings correspond to the amount and weight of the goods stored, as well as to the height of the racking. Because of their high ceilings, heavy distribution facilities also have the potential for two-story office buildout, which is independent from the distribution and warehouse functions.

WAREHOUSE DISTRIBUTION

HEAVY DISTRIBUTION/ EVOLUTION

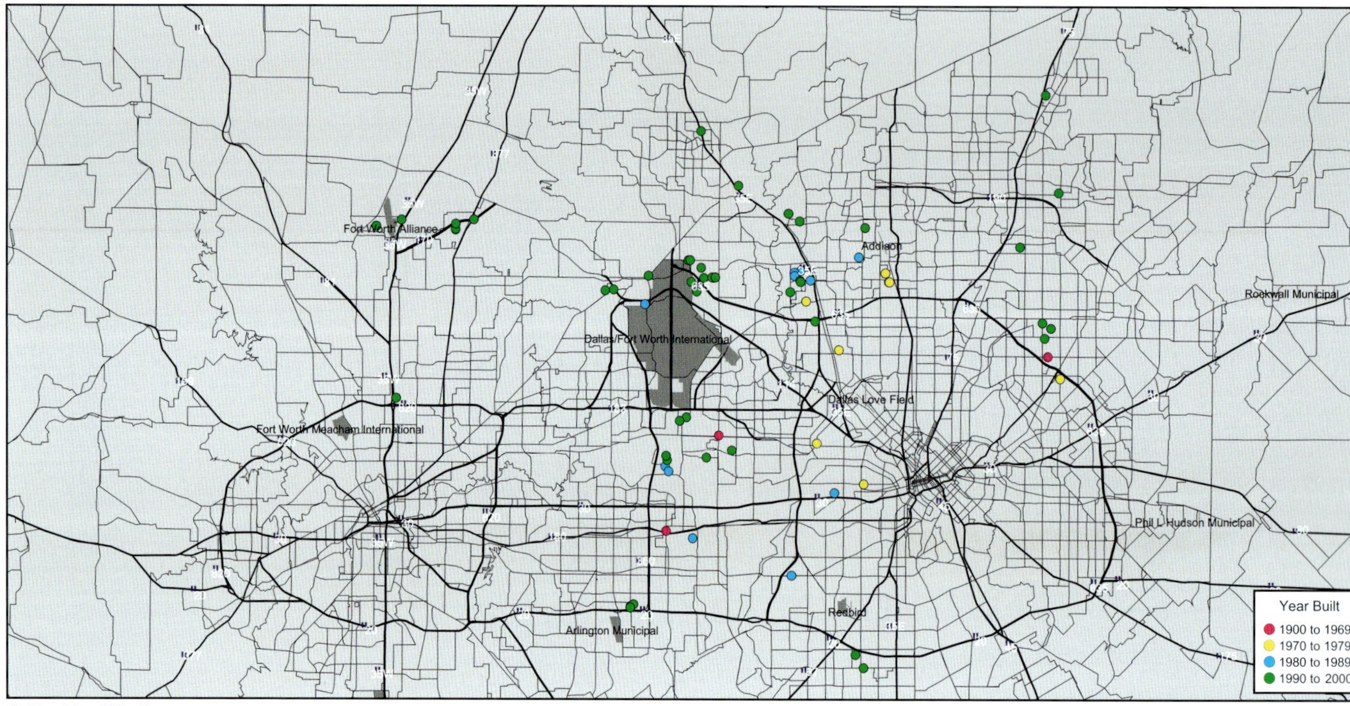

Dallas/Fort Worth.

The range of tenants is more restricted in heavy distribution facilities than in bulk warehouse facilities because of the emphasis on distribution rather than warehousing. Heavy distribution buildings often house logistics companies that engage in rapid just-in-time distribution activities, and they may be referred to as "high-velocity facilities" based on that function.

Heavy distribution facilities are the second-newest and the least numerous building type in the warehouse distribution category, following rack-supported buildings. (See the air cargo evolution section for a hybrid type combining features of heavy distribution and air cargo buildings.)

In the accompanying map depicting 74 heavy distribution buildings in the Dallas/Fort Worth market, two patterns are apparent. The first is the dominance of heavy distribution buildings constructed in the 1990s, indicated by green dots. Of the sample, nearly 70 percent were constructed during that period, only 4 percent were built before 1970, and the remainder were built in the 1980s.

A second pattern evident in the Dallas/Fort Worth example is the evolution of location. Newer buildings are located farther from the metropolitan center, which is consistent with the evolutionary pattern of the warehouse distribution category overall. Unlike regional and bulk warehouses, however, heavy distribution buildings are not generally located within the center of the metropolitan area.

REFRIGERATED DISTRIBUTION

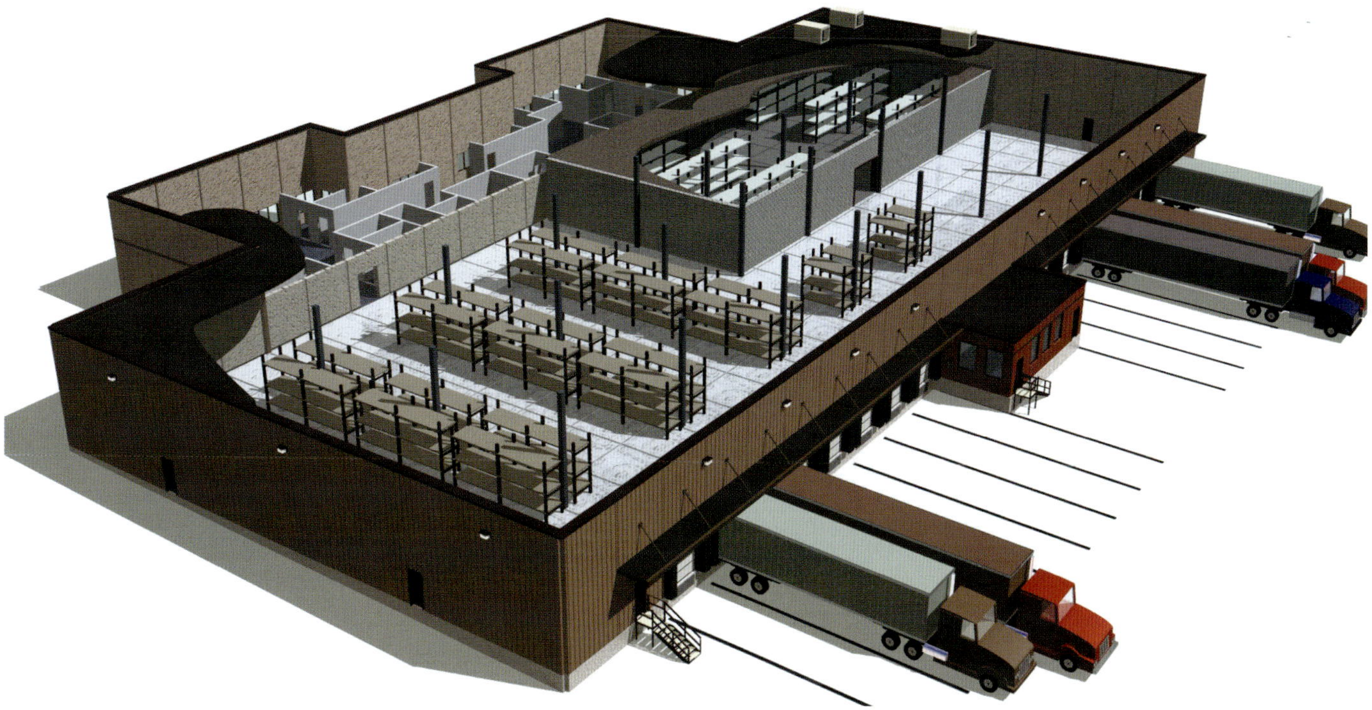

There are relatively few refrigerated distribution buildings because of their specialized function. Perishable goods are stored in these buildings for only short periods of time, and the focus is on distribution, rather than storage, of products.

Refrigerated distribution buildings resemble warehouse buildings from the exterior, but they have clear identifying interior features. Freezers and wheel-in coolers are found in other types of warehouses and some manufacturing and freight-forwarding buildings, but in refrigerated distribution buildings they are incorporated into the design of the building. Because cooling features are an integrated part of the building, converting refrigerated distribution buildings to other types of warehouse distribution facilities is generally not economical, although in certain cases, the freezer floor can be used as a standard floor.

WAREHOUSE DISTRIBUTION

REFRIGERATED DISTRIBUTION/ EXTERIOR

Refrigerated distribution buildings constitute the only warehouse distribution category with no size restriction. In fact, identifying these buildings from the exterior can be difficult because they vary so greatly in square footage. For example, in Chicago these types of buildings range from 5,000 to nearly 900,000 square feet.

Refrigerated distribution buildings are distinguished from other warehouse building types by the use of interior docks, which are warranted by the type of goods stored. In some facilities the entire interior dock area is temperature-controlled. In addition, the exterior docks are usually weather-sealed to minimize the exposure of products to outdoor temperatures. The number of square feet per dock rarely exceeds 10,000; the average is 7,000 to 8,000 square feet to one dock.

Refrigerated distribution buildings typically occupy 50 percent of the total site; the remaining 50 percent of space is used for parking and truck courts. This ratio is the result of a lower car-parking requirement and the infrequent need for trailer storage. The ratio is similar to that of bulk and regional warehouses.

REFRIGERATED DISTRIBUTION/ INTERIOR

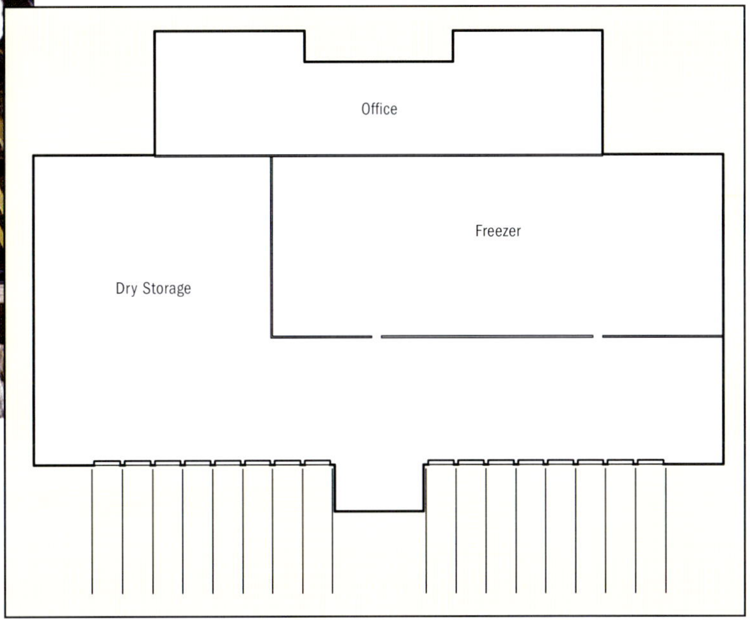

Refrigerated distribution buildings have a unique interior physical design that generally consists of four sections. Two sections account for a minimum of 25 percent of the building: a freezer floor section, which is integrated into the building structure; and a cooler, in which the temperature is maintained typically just above freezing. A third section—dry storage—is present in warehouses that store more than one type of goods, which applies to most refrigerated distribution buildings. A fourth section is allocated to office buildout. Large refrigerated distribution buildings have minimal office space of about 5 percent; smaller facilities have as much as 15 percent devoted to office buildout. An additional processing area, not exceeding 10 percent of the entire structure, which also can be cooled, is found in some food buildings. Buildings with large processing areas and small freezer and cooler areas are classified in the manufacturing category.

The freezer capability of refrigerated distribution facilities calls for additional requirements not needed in other warehouse distribution categories—heavy power, dual sprinkler systems, floor drains, and special loading features. Different types of sprinkler systems are present in the cold and dry/office areas.

Ceiling height varies according to building size. Refrigerated distribution buildings that exceed 50,000 square feet have ceiling heights ranging from 16 feet to more than 30 feet. Facilities smaller than 10,000 square feet have slightly lower ceilings.

WAREHOUSE DISTRIBUTION

REFRIGERATED DISTRIBUTION/ EVOLUTION

The most common tenants of refrigerated distribution facilities are food-processing and distribution companies. The accompanying map shows the location of 19 refrigerated distribution buildings in the Chicago market. This limited sample does not provide enough data for analysis of evolutionary patterns.

Similar small samples collected in other major industrial markets indicate that the average age of refrigerated distribution buildings is consistent throughout markets and more closely approximates that of buildings in the manufacturing category than that of buildings in warehouse distribution. The average age pattern is illustrated on the accompanying map. Although a small sample, this pattern indicates a lack of new demand for this building type. The refrigerated distribution category does not include manufacturing buildings, which also have freezers and coolers. It is important, therefore, not to assume the same level of demand for manufacturing food-processing facilities as for refrigerated distribution facilities.

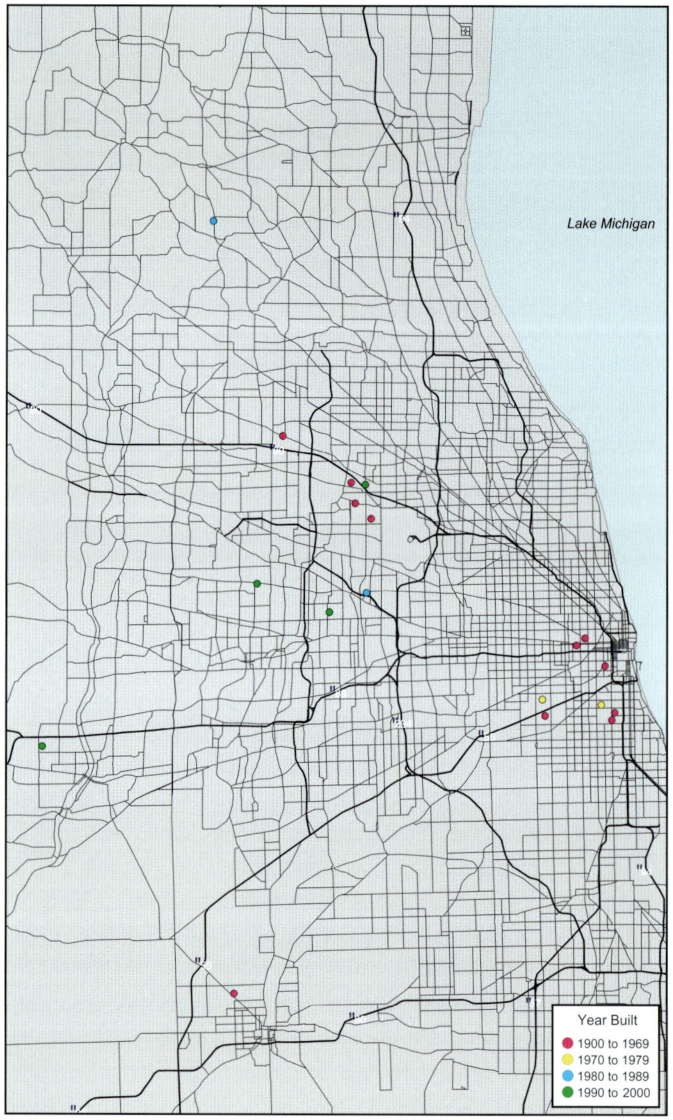

Chicago.

RACK-SUPPORTED WAREHOUSE

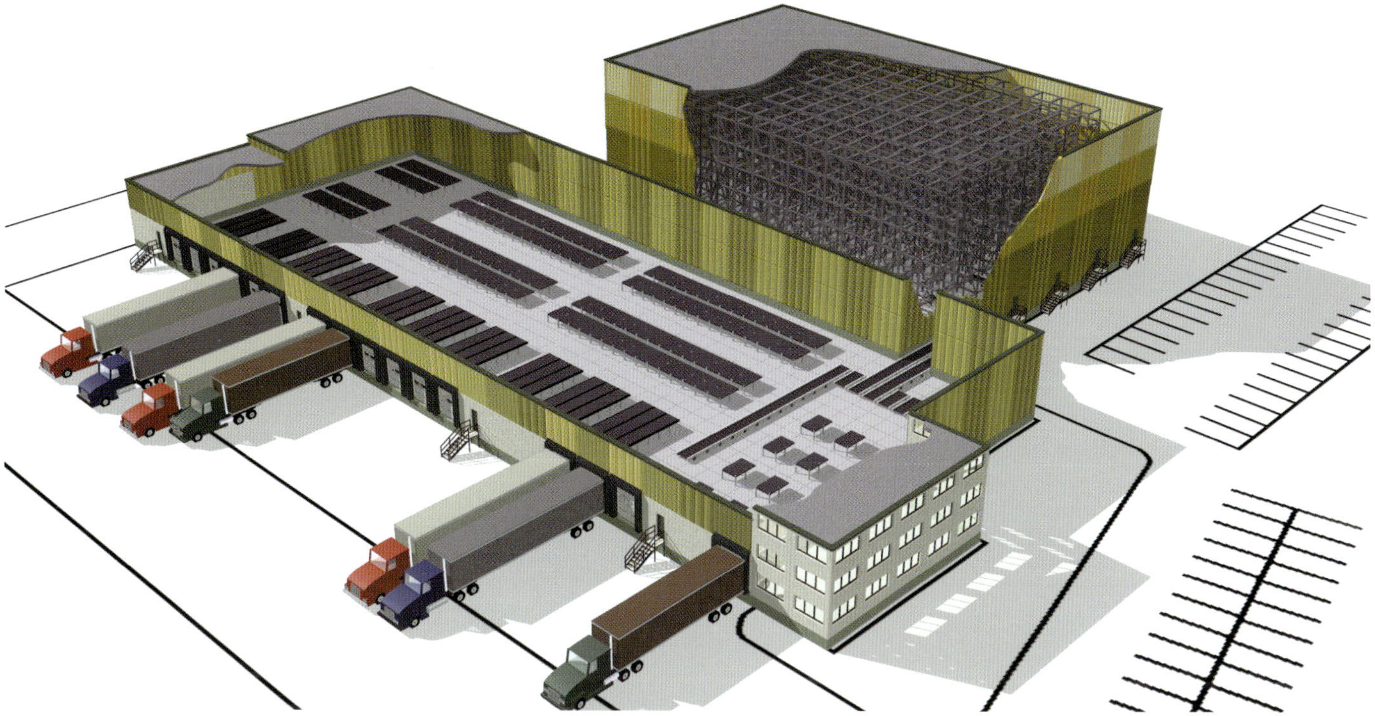

Rack-supported warehouses are the least common type of warehouse in the United States. These buildings lack flexibility and are relatively expensive to build, but because they are space-efficient, they are more frequently constructed in certain locations in Europe and Asia, where the cost of land is much higher. Their unique external and internal characteristics justify the classification of these buildings as a separate warehouse distribution category.

"Rack-supported" aptly describes the physical structure of these facilities. In traditional warehouses, the walls and roofs have separate support columns. In rack-supported buildings, the racking system provides both structural support and storage space, with the advantage of a more efficient use of space. For developers, a disadvantage of rack-supported buildings is that they are built to suit for specific user size and load needs. If either the size or load requirements change, the building loses its specific usefulness.

Rack-supported buildings are uniquely configured with separate storage and shipping areas. The storage area has high ceilings and is filled with racking systems. The shipping area resembles a standard warehouse with loading docks and lower ceiling heights. The storage and shipping areas typically are connected by an automated conveyor system.

WAREHOUSE DISTRIBUTION

RACK-SUPPORTED WAREHOUSE/ EXTERIOR

Because of its separate storage and shipping areas, a rack-supported building often appears to be two adjacent buildings, each with different height and loading characteristics. Since rock-supported buildings generally are built to suit, the size of the buildings and their sites depends upon user needs, for which there are no set standards. Their high-volume interior design and the fact that docks or truck courts are located only in the shipping area mean that these facilities require the least land per square foot of building space of any warehouse distribution building. The entire warehouse operation is automated, requiring fewer workers, so the number of employees per square foot in rack-supported buildings is the smallest of all warehouse types—which results in lower parking requirements and the possibility of using more site area for building coverage rather than parking lots. As a result, the site coverage for these buildings is the highest of all warehouse buildings. There is no meaningful square-footage-to-dock ratio for the entire building, but in the shipping area it can be as low as 5,000 to one.

RACK-SUPPORTED WAREHOUSE/ INTERIOR

The storage and loading sections in rack-supported buildings have entirely different physical characteristics. The storage area consists of racking supporting walls and roof cladding. With no support columns, space is maximized and elevated ceilings, as high as 78 feet, are possible. High ceilings and racking systems create special demands on floor stability and levelness. External forces, such as wind and snow load, also require special consideration.

The warehousing operation in these buildings usually is completely automated. Tall, computer-operated stacker cranes lift, pull, or grab stored units. Automated conveyer belts connect the storage and loading areas, and employees within this area perform mostly routine functions. The loading area has traditional wall and roof support, and is designed for sorting, labeling, grouping, and dispatching goods taken from the storage area. A section of this area is usually designated for office buildout.

WAREHOUSE DISTRIBUTION

RACK-SUPPORTED WAREHOUSE/ EVOLUTION

With only a limited number of rack-supported facilities in the United States, no expansion pattern for them has been established. Because they have fully automated transport and retrieval systems, their construction typically follows advances in the field of logistics.

This building type is much more prominent in Europe and Asia, in cities where land prices justify their high construction costs. Although land is generally much more readily available in the United States, the cost and the time required for the approvals process for greenfield site development is increasing. Therefore, the popularity of rack-supported facilities may increase in certain dense U.S. markets in the future.

MANUFACTURING

Manufacturing is the second-largest primary category of industrial real estate, occupying approximately 30 percent, or 7 billion square feet, of industrial space in the United States. All manufacturing facilities have distinctive physical characteristics relating to the manufacturing processes that they house.

Interior space configuration is their most important core differentiating characteristic. Buildings contain three types of space: manufacturing, warehouse, and office. Manufacturing space accounts for at least 50 percent, with an average close to 70 percent. Certain multitenant and research and development (R&D) flex buildings are built out with a comparable amount of manufacturing space, but the high proportion of manufacturing space is a core requirement of manufacturing facilities; that feature differentiates them from all other industrial real estate, including multitenant and R&D flex.

Heavy power, which is required for the heavy machinery used in the manufacturing process, is present in all manufacturing buildings and is a core feature differentiating these facilities. Data switch centers have an equal power requirement, but their level of power currently is greater on a per-square-foot basis than in manufacturing facilities.

Manufacturing buildings have a number of additional core and ancillary differentiating features. The exterior features are minimal provisions for loading and a high ratio of car parking per square foot. Heavy floor load capacity and provisions for cranes are interior features. These features create significant variation among manufacturing facilities. The manufacturing primary category, therefore, has three distinct secondary categories: light manufacturing, heavy manufacturing, and airport hangar. Each category houses manufacturing or manufacturing-related functions, such as assembly and maintenance, but each has unique differentiating physical characteristics.

MANUFACTURING

	SIZE (SQUARE FEET)	PERCENTAGE OFFICE	PERCENTAGE MANUFACTURING	CEILING HEIGHT	DOCK RATIO	RAIL	CRANE CAPACITY
LIGHT MANUFACTURING Light manufacturing is the most diverse building type within the manufacturing category and, therefore, the hardest to classify. Tenant use is also varied. The spectrum ranges from buildings that are greatly similar to warehouse buildings, to true manufacturing facilities that resemble heavy manufacturing buildings.	Up to 300,000	Up to 20%	50%–75%	14'–24'	1: 10,000–15,000	Occasionally: Exterior	Up to 25 tons
HEAVY MANUFACTURING Size, loading capability, and interior space buildout differentiate heavy manufacturing from other building types. Heavy manufacturing processes require multiple modes of transportation and the use of heavy-duty machinery. Rail service and trucks provide the exterior, while cranes the interior transportation. Heavy power and floor loads accommodate the heavy-duty machinery.	Can exceed 1 million	Averages 10%	75%–90%	16'–60'	Varies	Frequently: Interior and Exterior	Can exceed 100 tons
AIRPORT HANGAR Like warehouse distribution facilities, airport hangars store a product (airplanes). Unlike warehouse distribution facilities, which warehouse and distribute goods, airport hangars perform repair and maintenance. For this reason, airport hangars are classified within the manufacturing primary category.	Any	5%	75%–90% Repair space	Up to 100'	Minimal	No	Variable

LIGHT MANUFACTURING

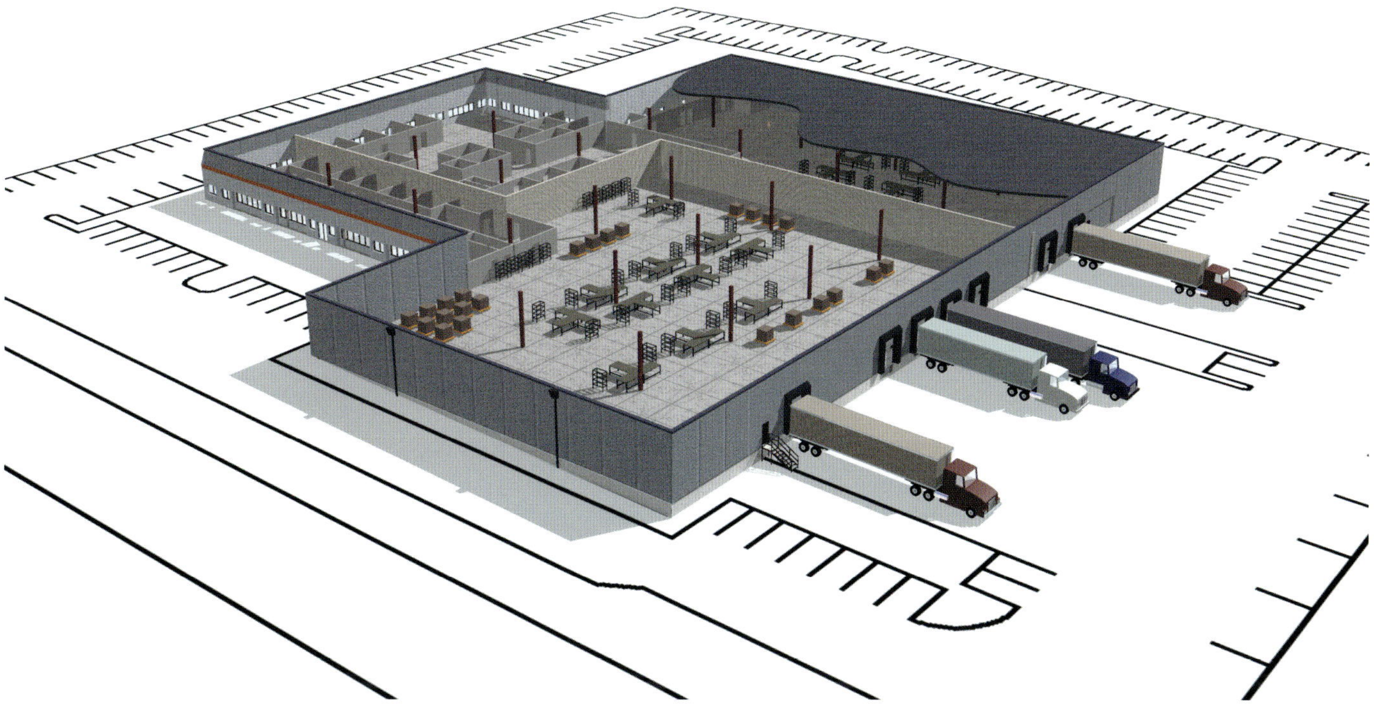

Light manufacturing is the most diverse building type within the manufacturing category and, therefore, the hardest to classify. Types of tenants are also varied. As a result, an examination of both exterior and interior features is necessary in order to classify this building type.

Light manufacturing buildings have more car parking and lower site coverage than warehouse distribution buildings, as well as a higher average ratio of square feet of space per dock. That higher average ratio can be misleading in identifying light manufacturing buildings because of an overlap in loading requirements between light manufacturing and warehouse distribution.

Average light manufacturing buildings have ceiling heights similar to those of regional warehouses (16 to 24 feet) and a building size similar to that of bulk warehouses (more than 100,000 square feet). Loading requirements, power, and buildout are identifying features of light manufacturing buildings.

MANUFACTURING

LIGHT MANUFACTURING/ EXTERIOR

Light manufacturing buildings are smaller in size than heavy manufacturing facilities. In general, light manufacturing buildings do not exceed 300,000 square feet, the average size of heavy manufacturing buildings. Buildings smaller than 100,000 square feet are usually classified as light rather than heavy manufacturing.

The loading facilities associated with light manufacturing buildings are both similar to and different from those in other types of manufacturing facilities. The use of both truck and rail transport is a feature shared with other manufacturing facilities, but light manufacturing buildings rely significantly less on rail transport than do heavy manufacturing buildings.

With a higher frequency of product flow than any other manufacturing category and greater reliance on truck transport, the ratio of square feet to docks ranges from 10,000 to 15,000 square feet per one dock in light manufacturing buildings, which is similar to that of some warehouse distribution buildings.

Light manufacturing buildings have average site coverage of 40 percent or slightly less because of the high car-parking requirement, which corresponds to the employment needs of light manufacturing and assembly tenants. This site coverage is lower than that of heavy manufacturing and most warehouse distribution buildings, but not as low as R&D flex.

MANUFACTURING

LIGHT MANUFACTURING/ INTERIOR

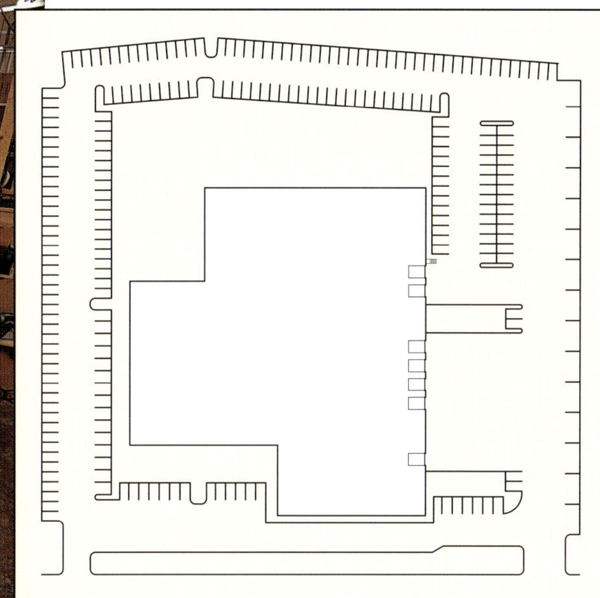

The lower ceiling heights of light manufacturing buildings—typically ranging from 14 to 24 feet—distinguish them from both heavy manufacturing facilities and warehouse distribution buildings. Less than 15 percent of all light manufacturing facilities feature ceiling heights outside this range.

Light manufacturing facilities include three types of space: manufacturing, warehouse, and office. On average, 50 to 75 percent of space is dedicated to manufacturing. The remaining 25 to 50 percent is allocated to warehouse and office space. Office buildout rarely exceeds 20 percent of an entire building. Light manufacturing buildings are commonly divided into multiple units.

When rail service is used, it generally does not enter the building, so there is less need for cranes. When used, crane capacity generally does not exceed 25 tons, well below the weight in heavy manufacturing buildings.

Like all manufacturing buildings, light manufacturing facilities have high power requirements. Their average power requirement is 2,000 amperes, which is midrange between the requirements of warehouse distribution and heavy manufacturing buildings.

MANUFACTURING

LIGHT MANUFACTURING/ EVOLUTION

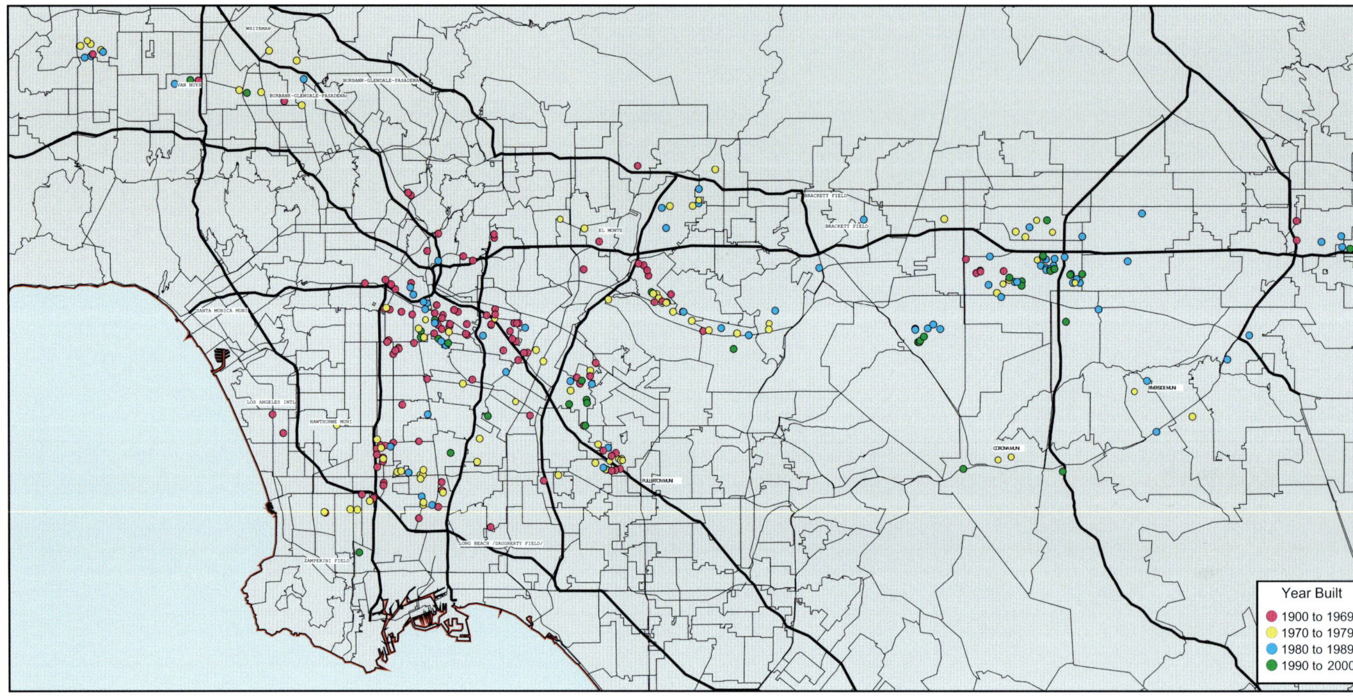

Los Angeles.

Because of their functional flexibility—the ability to house manufacturing, warehousing, and distribution functions—light manufacturing buildings are more common than any other type of manufacturing facility. Unlike the specialized construction of heavy manufacturing and airport hangar facilities, light manufacturing buildings demonstrate variety of design.

The accompanying map depicts 392 light manufacturing buildings in the Los Angeles market. In contrast to other types of manufacturing buildings, buildings in general are newer: 32 percent were built before 1970; 31 percent were built in the 1980s. The average year of construction for these facilities is 1975.

Light manufacturing buildings are built in clusters, a pattern that is driven by zoning restrictions and the need to be accessible to labor. Most light manufacturing buildings are built in proximity to other buildings of the same type, resulting in few isolated facilities. This geographic pattern is similar in other markets, such as Chicago and Denver.

Light manufacturing buildings most likely will remain the predominant type of manufacturing building. In the future, these buildings will continue to be developed with increased physical flexibility to fulfill both manufacturing and distribution functions, which would align them with warehouse distribution facilities. One example is Dell Computer Corporation's Parmer Lane North manufacturing plant in Austin, Texas. This 300,000-square-foot facility was initially intended to warehouse, but it now assembles and distributes products directly to consumers.

MANUFACTURING

HEAVY MANUFACTURING

Heavy manufacturing facilities typify the manufacturing category because of their large physical size and the heavy-duty manufacturing processes they house. Their function is to accommodate tenants that manufacture parts and finished products. Assembly is performed mostly in light manufacturing facilities.

Although heavy and light manufacturing buildings are closely related, size, loading capability, and interior space buildout differentiate them from one another. Heavy manufacturing buildings vary greatly in size, according to the building's use. They have high ceilings. The heavy manufacturing processes require multiple modes of transportation and use heavy-duty machinery. Rail service and trucks provide the exterior transportation. Cranes typically move materials on the inside. Because of the heavy-duty machinery, these facilities also require high power availability and floor-load capacity. Both the power and floor load ranges exceed those of light manufacturing facilities.

MANUFACTURING

HEAVY MANUFACTURING/ EXTERIOR

Heavy manufacturing buildings can be identified easily from the exterior. Because the buildings are designed primarily for heavy manufacturing activities, they are large and distinctive structures. Their loading capacity is less significant than buildings used for warehouse and distribution operations, and they have no standard ratio of space to the number of docks, which varies from 100,000 square feet per dock to 10,000 square feet per dock. In some cases, heavy manufacturing facilities do not have docks, just drive-in doors. Most heavy manufacturing buildings utilize rail service. In some facilities, rail is situated alongside the building, and the building is fitted with rail doors. In other facilities, rail enters the building. The type of transport used and the needs of the manufacturer influence the number of docks present.

In general, heavy manufacturing buildings are very large: the average size is more than 300,000 square feet. Although there are facilities as small as 60,000 square feet, buildings larger than 1 million square feet are not uncommon, especially in larger metropolitan markets such as Chicago, Los Angeles, and northern New Jersey.

The site coverage ratio is higher for heavy manufacturing facilities than for light manufacturing buildings. The average ratio ranges from 40 to 50 percent. This greater site coverage is the result of fewer employees per square foot and lower parking requirements.

HEAVY MANUFACTURING/ INTERIOR

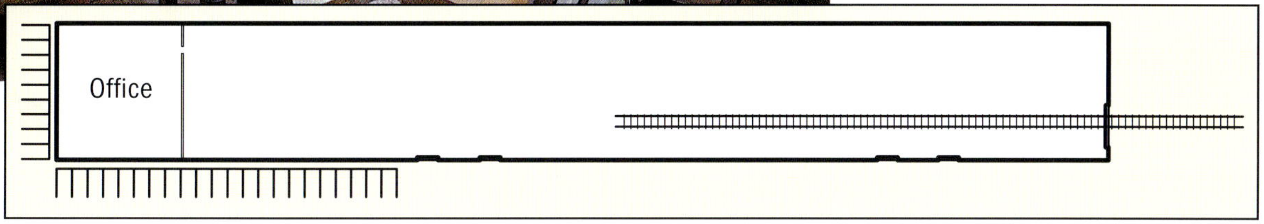

The interior of heavy manufacturing buildings is designed principally for its function. Up to 90 percent of space is dedicated to manufacturing, with the remainder allocated to office space. Rail service plays an important role in building layout, especially when interior rail must be accommodated. Typically, heavy manufacturing buildings have one or two tenants.

Heavy manufacturing facilities have the highest ceiling heights of all industrial real estate, with the exception of rack-supported buildings and airport hangars. The minimum ceiling height is 16 feet; the maximum height is around 60 feet. These high ceilings permit the construction of two-story office space within the building.

The presence and capacity of cranes is another differentiating feature. Although cranes are present in other manufacturing secondary categories, as well as in warehouse distribution facilities, the high capacity of cranes used in heavy manufacturing buildings is an identifying feature. Cranes with a capacity of more than 100 tons are common.

Requirements for heavy power and thick floors to support heavy equipment are two additional characteristics of heavy manufacturing facilities. For example, a typical building of 300,000 square feet with one crane can require up to 4,000 amperes and 480 volts. The largest buildings can have up to 9,000 amperes of power. Minimum floor thickness is six inches; eight inches is more common.

MANUFACTURING

HEAVY MANUFACTURING/ EVOLUTION

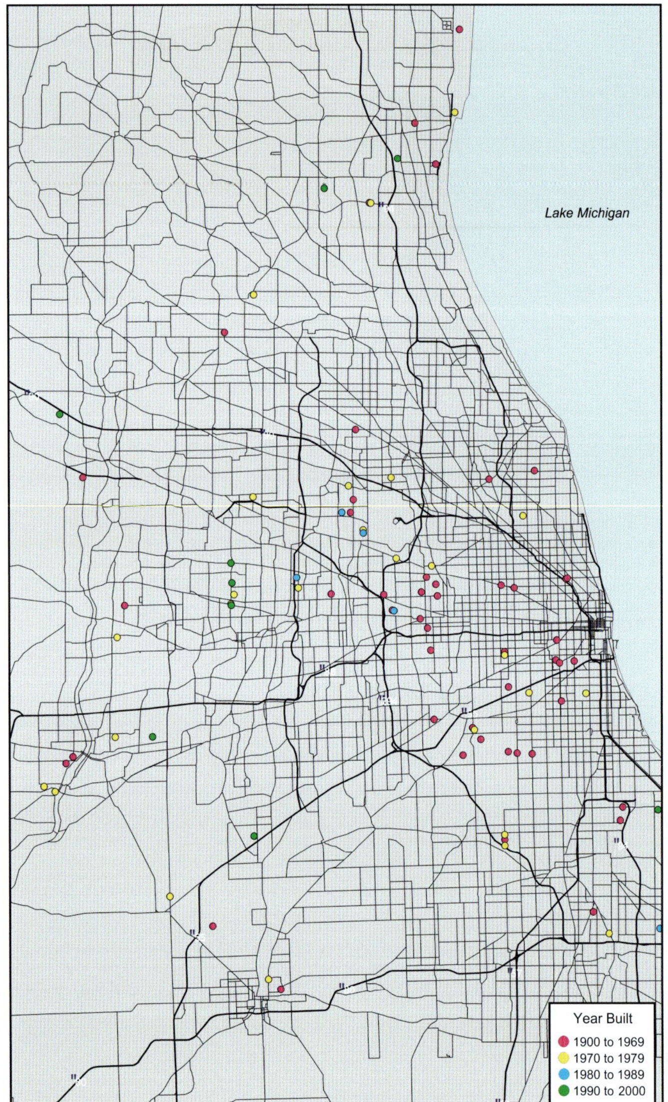

Chicago.

Heavy manufacturing buildings are used for a variety of functions, from processing raw materials to standard manufacturing of parts or even finished goods. The tenant type varies because of the vast range of use. Examples of heavy manufacturing tenants are U.S. Steel (steel production), General Motors Corporation (automobile production), and Motorola (wireless technology manufacture).

The accompanying map depicts the evolutionary pattern of heavy manufacturing facilities in the Chicago market. In general, heavy manufacturing buildings are the oldest type of industrial building; the number of buildings built before 1970 is significant. Of 109 buildings in this sample, 64 were constructed before 1970. Only 19 buildings were built after 1980. The average year of construction in this sample is 1961. Certain newer markets, such as Denver, have stock with a more recent average age of construction (1967). These data signify that construction of this facility type has been declining, a finding consistent with the national manufacturing employment trend. Manufacturing employment peaked in 1979, declined during the early 1980s, and has remained relatively flat since the manufacturing recession of 2002.

No significant geographic expansion pattern is associated with heavy manufacturing buildings. The location of these facilities depends heavily upon zoning and the availability of rail service, making clusters of buildings of all ages common.

AIRPORT HANGAR

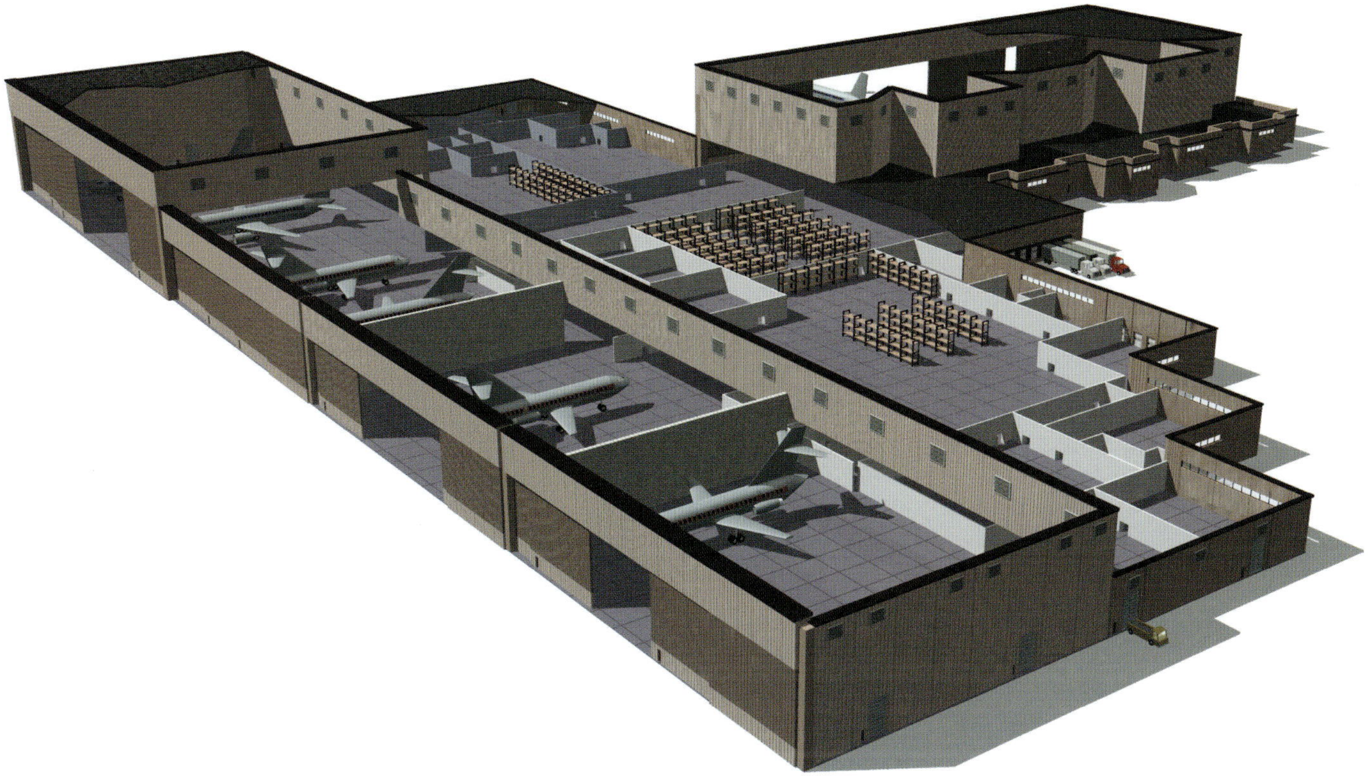

Like warehouse distribution facilities, airport hangars store a product. Unlike warehouse distribution facilities, which warehouse and distribute goods, airport hangars are used primarily for repair and maintenance. For this reason, airport hangars are classified in the manufacturing primary category.

Airport hangars are clearly identifiable because they must be large enough to accommodate an airplane. Their size corresponds to the type of aircraft they are designed to service; hangars that service commercial aircraft are similar in size to heavy manufacturing buildings and are larger and higher than most other industrial building types. Their ceiling heights meet and, in certain cases, exceed those of rack-supported buildings.

The interior buildout of airport hangars is complex. In addition to the aircraft section, a commercial hangar has multiple workshops, storage areas, and a separate area built out as offices. There is also a shipping and receiving area with several docks.

MANUFACTURING

AIRPORT HANGAR/ EXTERIOR

Airport hangars exist as individual buildings, as well as in complexes of several hangars with office, shop, and storage space. Their overall size depends on their configuration as well as on the size of the aircraft they maintain. Because airport hangars are located on airport grounds, no site coverage ratio is associated with this building type. Because of their unique location, car parking is not a meaningful differentiating feature.

Airport hangars have loading docks, especially in a multibuilding complex. These docks are used for the delivery of airplane parts and materials. Because the number of docks is minimal, there is no meaningful square-foot-per-dock ratio.

Airport hangars have a unique front door through which the aircraft enters the building. Since airport hangars are built to size and do not significantly exceed the size of a commercial aircraft, the drive-in door can be the entire front wall of the building.

AIRPORT HANGAR/ INTERIOR

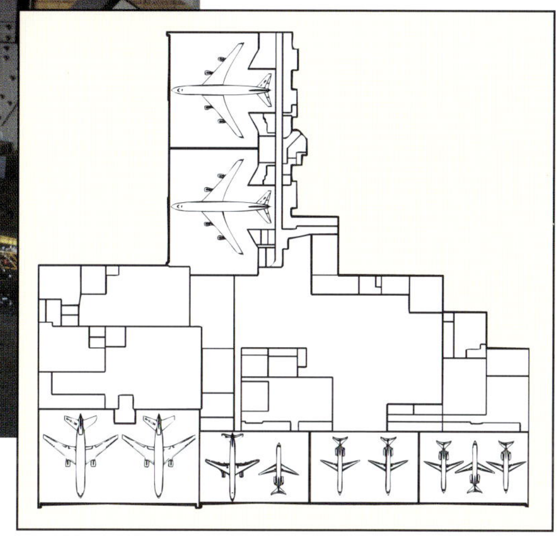

In a stand-alone airport hangar, most space is allocated to airplane storage and repair. In a multibuilding complex, airplane storage and repair constitute about half the entire area (see floor plan above right). The remaining space comprises shops, storage areas, and an office section. Airport hangars serve as repair facilities; therefore, the range of specialty shops is diverse and commonly includes sheet metal, machine, cowl, galley, composite, and carpet shops. Special buildout for paint booths is also sometimes present.

Like building size, ceiling height corresponds to the type and size of the airplane for which the hangar is designed. Facilities designed for the largest airplanes, BA 747s, have the highest ceilings, reaching almost 100 feet. Smaller commercial hangars have ceiling heights of 57 feet, which is still higher than that of almost all other industrial building types. Ceilings in the shop and office areas range from 12 to 32 feet.

MANUFACTURING

AIRPORT HANGAR/ EVOLUTION

Because airport hangars are located at airports, these facilities do not have an independent geographic expansion pattern. Tenants are companies that operate airlines and they have very specialized location requirements. Similar to many other types of industrial facilities, these buildings have become more upscale in appearance in recent years.

FLEX

Flex is the third-largest primary category of industrial real estate, representing approximately 9 percent—or 2 billion square feet—of the total supply of industrial real estate in the United States. Because the variation among flex facilities is subtle, they are difficult to categorize. The different names that refer to flex facilities reflect their diversity: flex, R&D/flex, R&D/flex/ showroom, flex tech, and service center/R&D flex. These names all refer to flexible buildings that can accommodate technology and service tenants. Flexibility of interior space configuration and an attractive exterior are core features differentiating flex facilities from other industrial building types. A relatively high proportion of office buildout also distinguishes these buildings as flex and differentiates them from other industrial facilities such as warehouse distribution or manufacturing.

An attractive external physical appearance, or high curb appeal, is an integral feature of flex facilities. Use of high-quality materials, abundant glass, and attractive landscaping creates an upscale appearance. On the interior, these buildings offer maximum flexibility in terms of space configuration and use. Two buildings that are identical from the exterior can have entirely different interior space buildouts. One facility can accommodate laboratory, high-tech manufacturing space, and office. Another facility can be configured with 90 percent office and 10 percent warehouse buildout. The interior configurations and the amount of office space provided vary widely by market. A higher percentage of office buildout is common in those metropolitan markets with low office vacancies and high office rents.

The amount of office space in flex buildings ranges from 25 to 80 percent. Flex facilities with 100 percent office buildout do exist; however, they are rare and stretch the boundaries of industrial real estate.

The flex primary category has two secondary categories—R&D flex and office showroom—that vary significantly. Both, however, have the three core differentiating features associated with flex facilities: high curb appeal, flexible design, and a high percentage of office space.

FLEX

	SIZE (SQUARE FEET)	PERCENTAGE OFFICE	PERCENTAGE HIGH-TECH SPACE/LAB	PERCENTAGE WAREHOUSE	CEILING HEIGHT	DOCK RATIO	CURB APPEAL
R&D FLEX Some R&D flex facilities resemble low-scale offices from the exterior. Most of the space in R&D flex is used as either high-tech manufacturing/laboratory or office. Warehouse space is the least utilized buildout, which corresponds with the R&D flex low loading requirements and high ratio of 20,000 square feet of space to one dock.	Up to 100,000	25%–75%	25%–75%	Below 20%	10'–18'	Averages 1: 20,000	High
OFFICE SHOWROOM Office showroom facilities and R&D flex buildings share certain common attributes. Office showrooms also resemble warehouses. However, the three core differentiating characteristics of the flex primary category—building flexibility, upscale appearance, and high office buildout—are present in all office showroom buildings.	Up to 150,000	30%–40%	0%	Up to 70%	16'–28'	1: 10,000	High

R&D FLEX

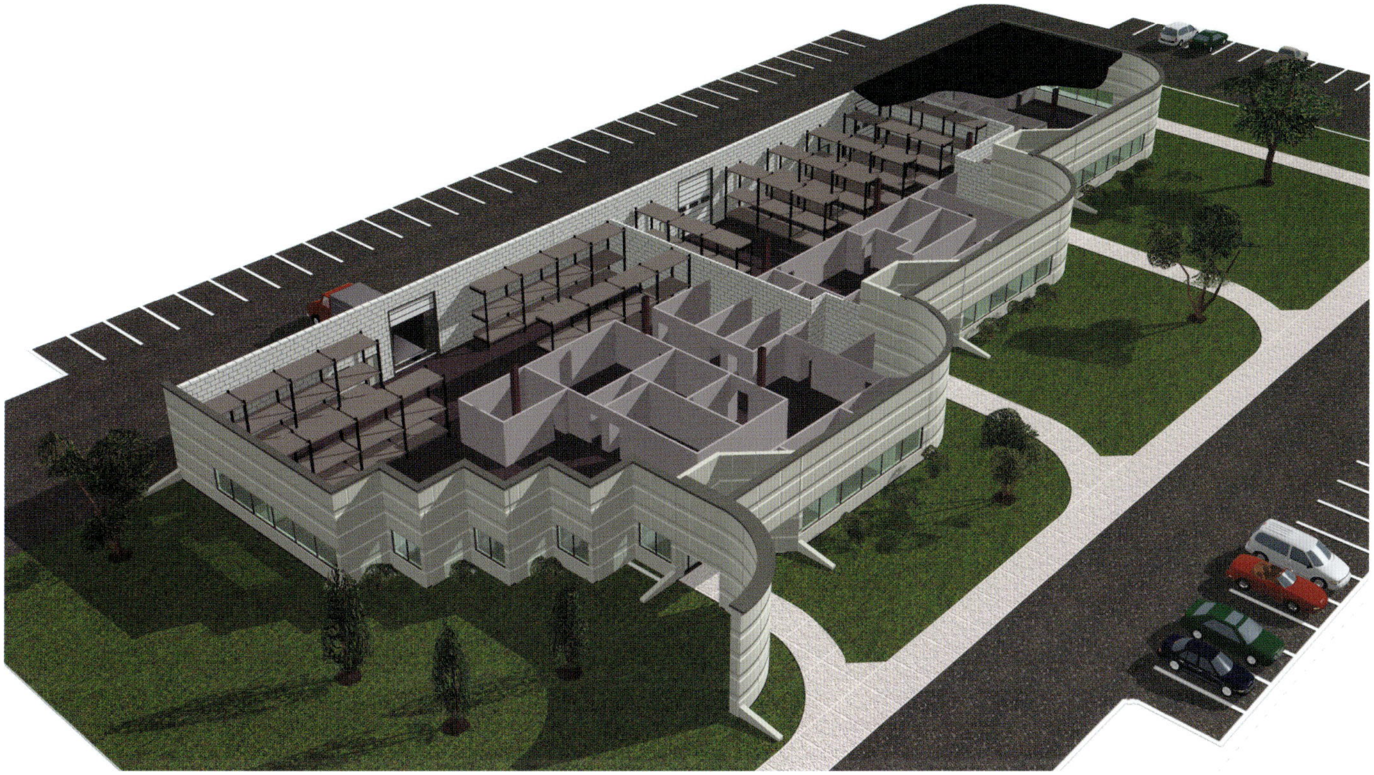

High-quality R&D flex buildings can be mistaken for low-scale office buildings from the outside, but the interiors are very different. The typical tenants of R&D flex facilities require a cleaner environment than do those of manufacturing and warehousing facilities. The volume of traffic is lower on R&D flex premises, and the vehicles are lighter. The result is less heavy truck presence, better roads, more extensive landscaping, and an overall officelike atmosphere.

R&D flex buildings range from 20,000 to 100,000 square feet and generally do not exceed 100,000 square feet. They are similar to multitenant buildings and regional warehouses in terms of size; however, their exterior appearance and interior space configuration classify them as flex buildings. Most space in R&D flex is used as either high-tech manufacturing/laboratory or office. This space can constitute as much as 75 percent of an entire building. Warehouse space is the least utilized buildout, corresponding to R&D flex's low loading requirements and high ratio of 20,000 square feet per dock.

FLEX

R&D FLEX/ EXTERIOR

R&D flex buildings are clearly distinguishable from the other industrial building types by their minimal loading requirements and high curb appeal. These characteristics contrast to most industrial real estate, which is commonly associated with the presence of loading facilities for heavy trucks and less attractive building facades.

Most R&D flex buildings have loading capability featuring either docks or, more commonly, drive-in doors. The ratio of square feet to docks is very high, with an average ratio for the R&D flex category of 20,000-plus square feet per dock. Larger facilities have only a few docks for an entire building: a ratio of 20,000 to 30,000 square feet per dock. Smaller buildings may have only one drive-in door, resulting in similar ratios.

R&D flex buildings have appealing facades that feature high-quality materials, more extensive use of glass, and an upgraded building entrance. Professionally landscaped, the sites often include trees, plants, and water features. Instead of truck courts and trailer parking, emphasis is placed on car parking. R&D flex buildings employ more individuals per square foot than light manufacturing buildings, thus requiring more car parking. Some R&D flex buildings match the car-parking requirements of office buildings: four automobile spaces per 1,000 square feet. This high parking requirement reduces the building's site coverage ratio to a range of 25 to 40 percent.

The size of the facility and number of stories are additional attributes of R&D flex facilities. They rarely exceed 100,000 square feet, and they are usually, but not always, configured as single-story structures.

FLEX

R&D FLEX/ INTERIOR

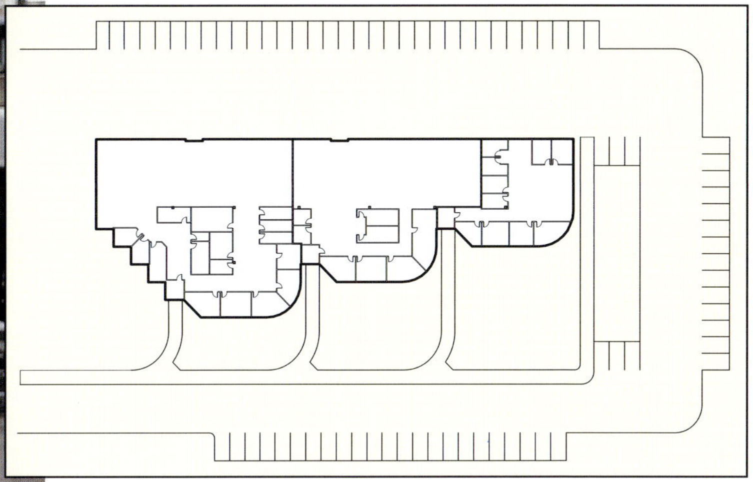

The interior design of R&D flex buildings is usually tailored to the needs of specific tenants. The minimum office buildout is 25 percent; the maximum buildout can exceed 70 percent. The remaining space is usually allocated among light manufacturing, laboratory/clean rooms, and warehouse space; however, these three types of space are not present in every R&D flex building. Most R&D flex buildings have multiple tenants, which requires additional space buildout.

Warehouse space can be as low as 5 percent of total buildout—the smallest space allocation in R&D flex buildings. The light manufacturing space is used differently from similar space in light manufacturing facilities. Whereas the manufacturing process involves heavy power, in R&D flex facilities it is oriented toward high-tech assembly, a process that is cleaner and uses different types of instruments. Laboratory/clean space, which requires a special buildout, is often present.

Low ceiling heights distinguish R&D flex buildings from other industrial facility types. Heights range from a minimum of 10 feet to a maximum of 18 feet. Average ceiling height ranges from 12 to 16 feet.

FLEX

R&D FLEX/ EVOLUTION

A number of technology companies use R&D flex facilities for developing, testing, and manufacturing their products. For this reason, R&D flex is the most technologically oriented of the industrial real estate categories. R&D flex buildings also can function with a 100 percent office buildout, especially during periods of tight office markets and high rents.

A newer category of industrial real estate than manufacturing and warehouse distribution, the oldest R&D flex buildings shown on the accompanying map of the Denver market were developed in the 1950s. The average year of construction for this sample is 1984, which is consistent with other major industrial markets. Of note is that almost 60 percent of the Denver sample was completed during the construction boom of the 1980s.

R&D flex buildings exist in clusters of both new and old buildings. For this reason, R&D flex buildings display a growth pattern that is similar to that of manufacturing buildings. Most major industrial markets have a submarket with more R&D flex buildings than other areas that is driven by zoning and access to skilled labor.

In addition to R&D flex clusters, development of new mixed-use business parks has become common. These parks consist of diverse industrial building types and attract tenants that can benefit from synergies created by locating close to each other.

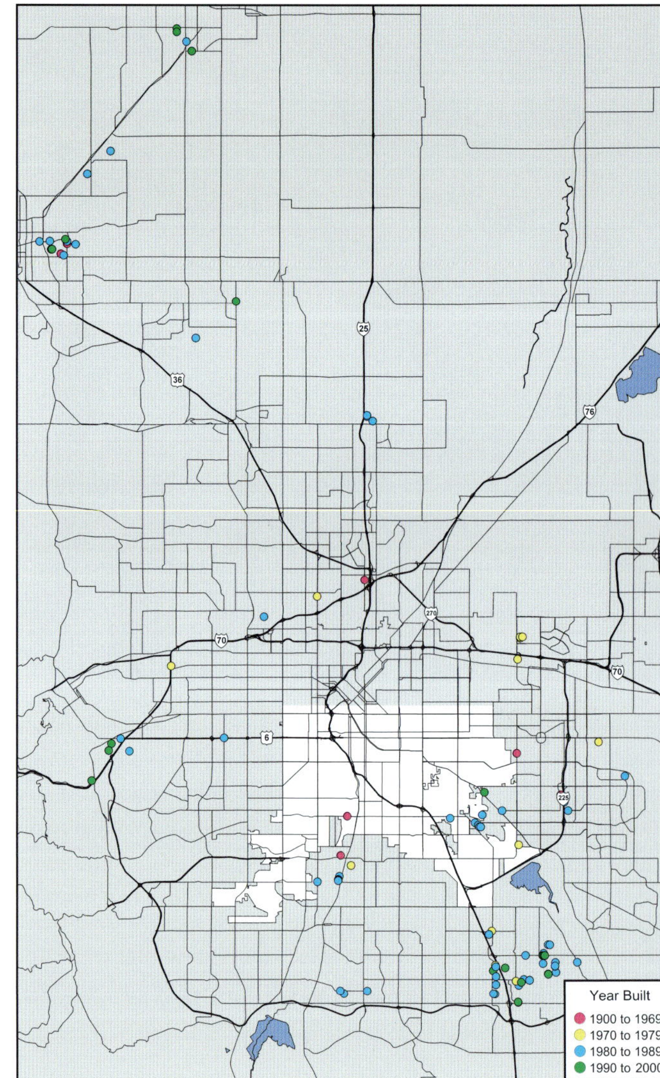

Denver.

OFFICE SHOWROOM

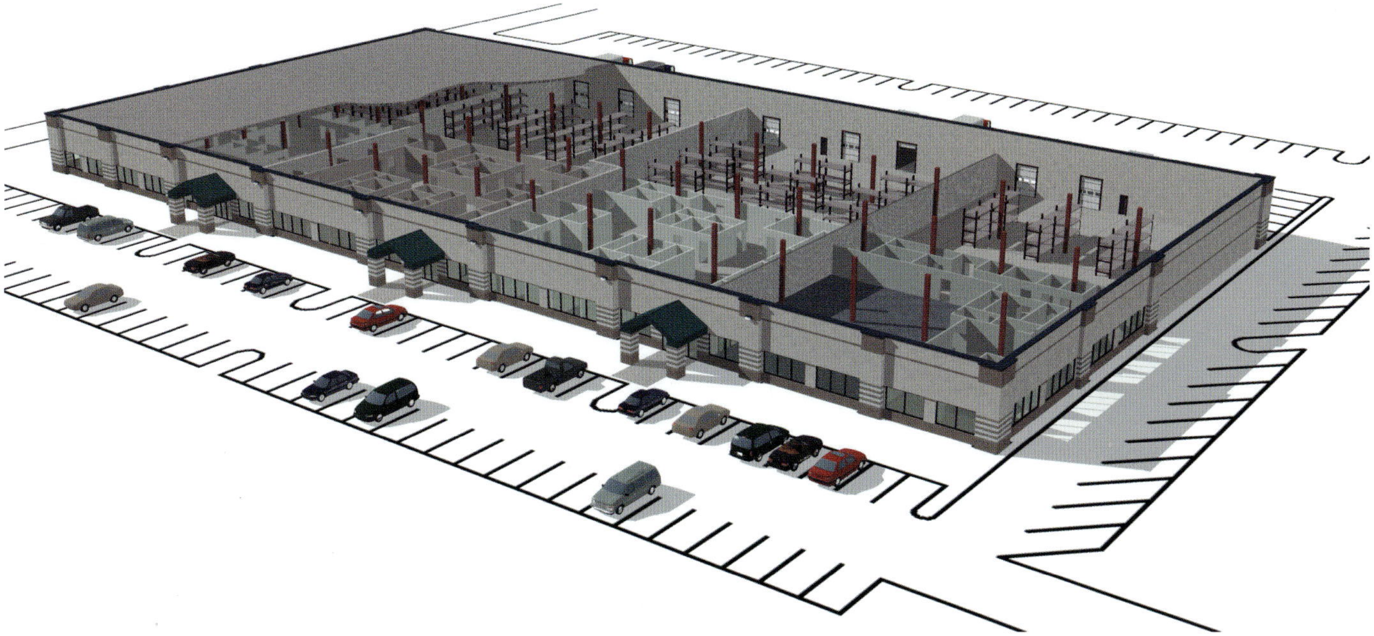

Office showroom facilities house a variety of functions. Generally 40 percent of the facility is allocated to office space, up to 60 percent is allocated to warehouse space, and up to 20 percent is dedicated to retail showroom space. This retail space component differentiates office showrooms from most other industrial property types. In fact, the term "showroom" connotes the potential for retail space buildout.

Office showroom facilities resemble R&D flex buildings but also share certain common attributes with warehouses. The high ceilings and low ratio of square feet to docks are factors that align these facilities more closely to the warehouse distribution category. High curb appeal, attractive landscaping, lower site coverage, and higher office buildout, however, classify office showrooms within the flex primary category.

The office showroom's shared attributes with both flex and warehouse distribution facilities require additional core variables to be identified for classification purposes. Upscale finishes are found at the front exterior of these buildings, while the back of the building has multiple loading docks and deep truck courts. The average ceiling height of office showrooms is 20 feet. This height distinguishes these buildings from R&D flex buildings and aligns them with warehouse distribution buildings.

FLEX

OFFICE SHOWROOM/ EXTERIOR

Like R&D flex buildings, office showrooms have an upscale appearance that differentiates them from regional warehouses. However, the loading capacity of office showrooms has entirely different specifications from that of R&D flex buildings and this feature aligns office showrooms with the warehouse distribution category as well.

An appealing exterior is necessary to encourage visitor and customer traffic when there is a retail component. In fact, office showrooms have more visitor traffic than any other type of industrial building. The back of the building, however, where loading takes place, resembles a warehouse. The average ratio of square feet to docks is approximately 10,000 to one, about one-half the ratio commonly found in R&D flex buildings, and in line with that of regional warehouses.

Office showroom building size generally ranges from 20,000 to 150,000 square feet, although buildings outside this size range exist. In comparison with R&D flex buildings, office showrooms have a slightly lower parking requirement: 2.5 spaces per 1,000 square feet. However, they require more land dedicated to loading: an average range of 30 to 40 percent site coverage, with 50 percent maximum. This ratio conforms to the flex primary category.

OFFICE SHOWROOM/ INTERIOR

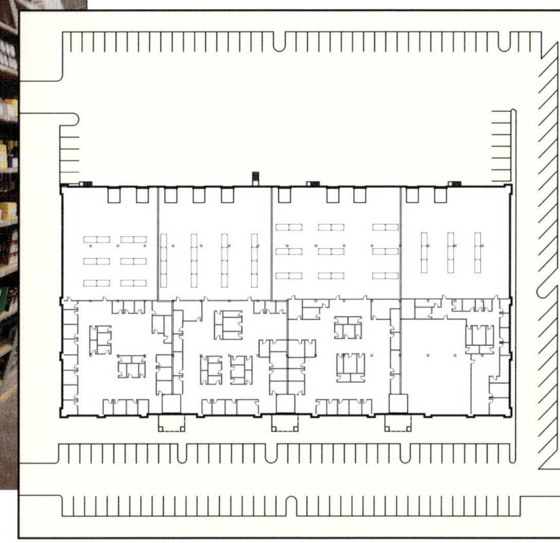

Office showrooms are frequently subdivided for multiple tenant use. They have a simpler interior space configuration than R&D flex buildings. Combined, office and warehouse space generally account for 80 percent in showrooms with a retail component. Office space ranges from 30 to 40 percent, which is approximately 15 percent higher than in standard regional warehouses. Buildout quality is also higher, which is consistent with the overall appearance of office showrooms.

The building height of office showrooms is directly related to the facility's partial warehouse function. The minimum ceiling height is 16 feet; the maximum height can reach 28 feet. The high ceiling height is visible in the warehouse section of the building only and the office area has dropped ceilings that approximate typical office levels.

OFFICE SHOWROOM/ EVOLUTION

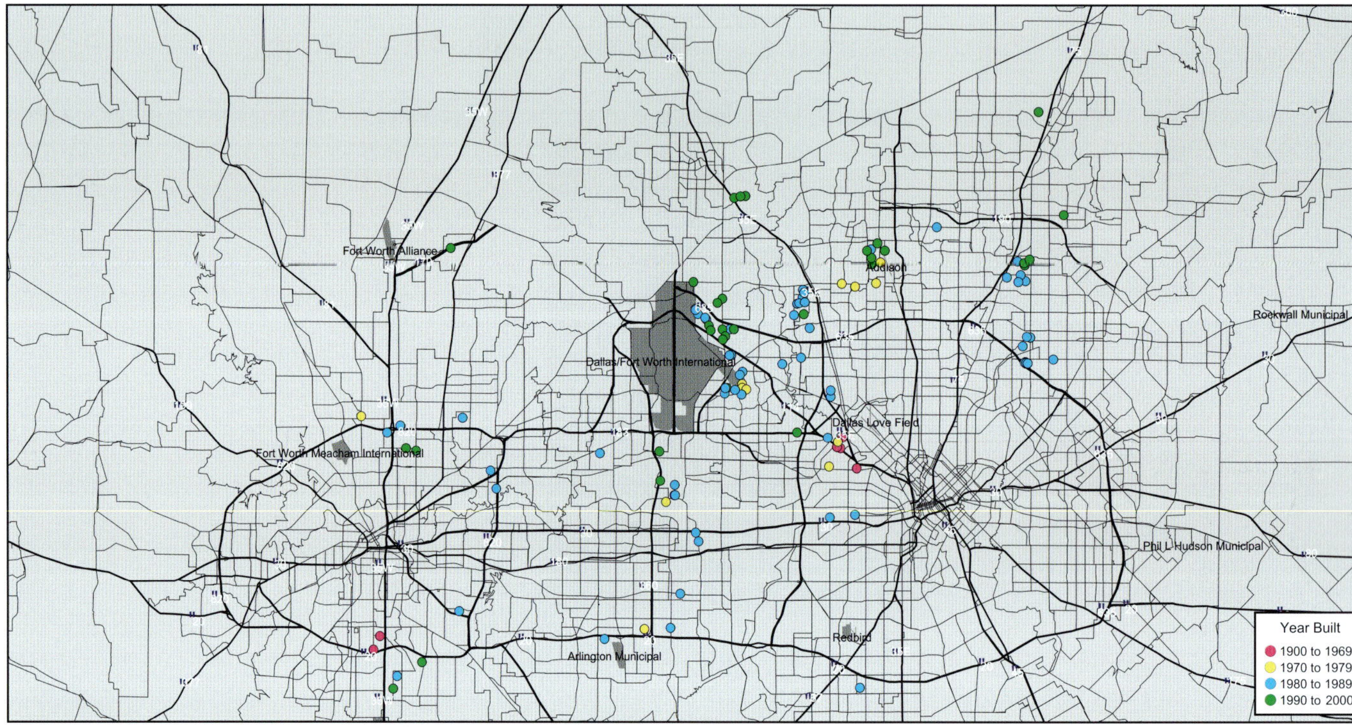

Dallas/Fort Worth.

The office showroom is a new flex secondary category. Its physical characteristics attract warehouse tenants that require attractive facilities, a higher percentage of office space, and, in certain cases, retail space.

The accompanying map depicts 127 office showrooms in the Dallas/ Fort Worth market. The majority of these buildings, 81 percent, were constructed after the 1980s. The average year of construction for office showrooms in the Dallas/ Fort Worth area is 1985. The high number of buildings constructed in this recent time frame is consistent with other U.S. markets. As a result, office showroom is the third-youngest industrial building type, following rack-supported and heavy distribution facilities.

Office showrooms and regional warehouses share a similar evolutionary pattern. Office showrooms follow population expansion patterns: newer buildings are located farther from the metropolitan center; older ones are situated closer to the city center. In comparison with R&D flex buildings, office showrooms are more restricted by zoning because of their warehouse function and resulting heavy truck presence.

MULTITENANT

Historically, multitenant facilities have not been classified as an independent category but have been grouped with either warehouses or manufacturing facilities. However, the physical characteristics of multitenant facilities differ from those of both warehouses and manufacturing facilities, justifying the creation of a separate multitenant primary classification category. Multitenant facilities are the most varied in use and tenant base of industrial real estate. The ability to house multiple tenants is a core attribute differentiating this category. Multitenant buildings also exhibit a unique combination of the characteristics of R&D flex, light manufacturing, and regional warehouse buildings.

Multitenant buildings provide small businesses the opportunity to lease varying amounts of space. Typical new tenants lease single, small units. As these tenants grow in size, so do their space needs, and they absorb adjacent units until they need to relocate to a larger type of facility. For this reason, multitenant buildings efficiently accommodate new, emerging, and small businesses. They also can accommodate established and older businesses, which may not experience significant growth.

A typical multitenant building accommodates a mix of light manufacturing and warehouse tenants. Because multitenant buildings are occupied by a number of smaller tenants, these facilities need to accommodate various activities. As a result, building use tends to differ from building to building, and from tenant unit to tenant unit. Warehouse distribution, manufacturing, flex, freight forwarding, and even data switch center buildings have multitenant configurations. The core differentiating feature of multitenant buildings, however, is a large number of smaller-sized tenants.

MULTITENANT

	SIZE (SQUARE FEET)	PERCENTAGE OFFICE	PERCENTAGE MANUFACTURING	CEILING HEIGHT	DOCK RATIO	SHAPE	OCCUPANCY
MULTITENANT A typical multitenant building is small in structure and designed in a nonrectangular shape. Multitenant buildings are configured in *L* and *U* shapes, although there are examples of numerous other shapes in every market. This flexible building type is ideal for multiple occupants. Most tenant space ranges from 5,000 to 15,000 square feet. Office buildout varies widely, in some cases exceeding 50 percent. The presence of space other than office and warehouse is dependent upon individual tenant needs.	Up to 120,000	Up to 50%	Up to 60%	16'–24'	Varies	Non-rectangular	Always multitenant

MULTITENANT

Multitenant buildings are among the most flexible types of industrial real estate, making them ideal for multiple occupants. Typically, a multitenant building is designed in a nonrectangular shape, such as an *L* or a *U*, although there are examples of numerous other shapes in every market.

Features that differentiate multitenant buildings from other facilities are related to the building's flexibility. A high percentage of office space, the presence of retail space, and significant variation in the use of space distinguish multitenant from regional warehouse facilities. The higher ceilings and lower curb appeal of multitenant buildings differentiate them from R&D flex buildings, and lower power requirements, better loading capabilities, and lower floor load distinguish them from light manufacturing buildings.

MULTITENANT

MULTITENANT/ EXTERIOR

Multitenant facilities are in the smaller range of industrial facilities, averaging about 80,000 square feet, with a maximum size of 120,000 square feet. Buildings smaller than 20,000 square feet also exist. Building shape varies from building to building. Unlike regional warehouses, multitenant buildings generally are not rectangular.

Loading capabilities including docks and drive-in doors can be shared or private, with as little as 4,000 square feet per dock or drive-in door. Because of the variety of multitenant building design, there are no standards or averages for loading capabilities. In some facilities, the square-foot-to-dock ratio approximates that of heavy distribution buildings. Other buildings have a few common docks that all tenants share. In both examples, the ratio of the number of docks per tenant is very low because of the high number of tenants per building. Some buildings have drive-in doors instead of, or in combination with, docks.

Facade treatments and landscaping are exterior features that distinguish multitenant buildings from R&D flex and office showroom facilities. Multitenant buildings commonly have loading in the front as well as in the back. The external physical image of the building is less appealing than that of flex buildings. The site tends to be maximized, which results in higher coverage ratios. Although a typical multitenant building has loading capabilities, goods move in low frequency and volume. The number of employees per square foot is also relatively low, although higher than in distribution-oriented buildings. As a result, multitenant buildings do not require truck courts as deep as those of warehouse distribution buildings, nor as much parking space as manufacturing and R&D flex buildings, which results in site-coverage ratios as high as 50-plus percent.

MULTITENANT/ INTERIOR

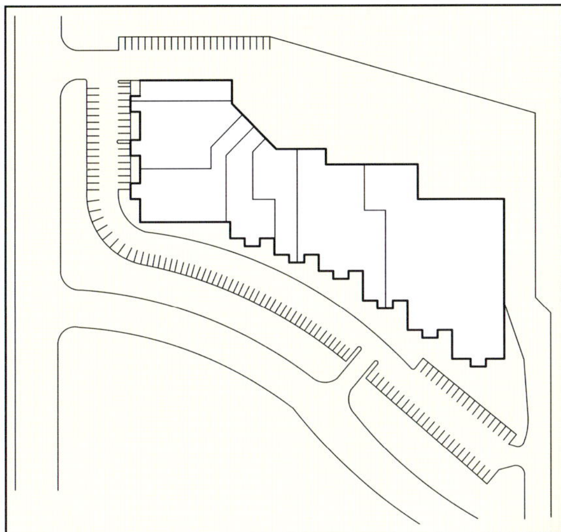

The average size of tenant units affects the overall size of a particular multitenant building. In general, a tenant unit ranges in size from 5,000 to 15,000 square feet, rarely exceeding 20,000 square feet or 25 percent of the entire structure. However, tenant units smaller than 3,000 square feet are not uncommon.

Space buildout in multitenant facilities varies from building to building and unit to unit. Office space is relatively high: 50 percent is not unusual. The high office buildout results from the fact that each tenant has a minimum office requirement regardless of the unit's size. Use of the remainder of the unit depends on a tenant's business and the building's capabilities. Space can be used for any combination of warehouse, showroom, manufacturing, and even telecommunications purposes.

The ceiling height of multitenant buildings ranges from 16 to 24 feet, midpoint between that of R&D flex and heavy distribution, and identical to that of regional warehouses.

MULTITENANT

MULTITENANT/ EVOLUTION

There is no typical tenant profile for multitenant facilities because of the versatility of the individual buildings. They can accommodate any type of business requiring a small amount of industrial space. Logistics companies do not lease multitenant facilities, however, because the buildings are not designed for distribution.

The accompanying map identifies 73 multitenant facilities in the Denver market. While warehouse distribution buildings follow the population expansion, and flex and manufacturing buildings concentrate in clusters, multitenant buildings of all ages are located both close in and farther out from the metropolitan center. Clustering is also minimal. This pattern is a result of the small size of the facilities and their versatility. Because multitenant buildings do not require any special conditions, such as access to major highways or fiber optic cable, this dispersed distribution pattern is expected to continue.

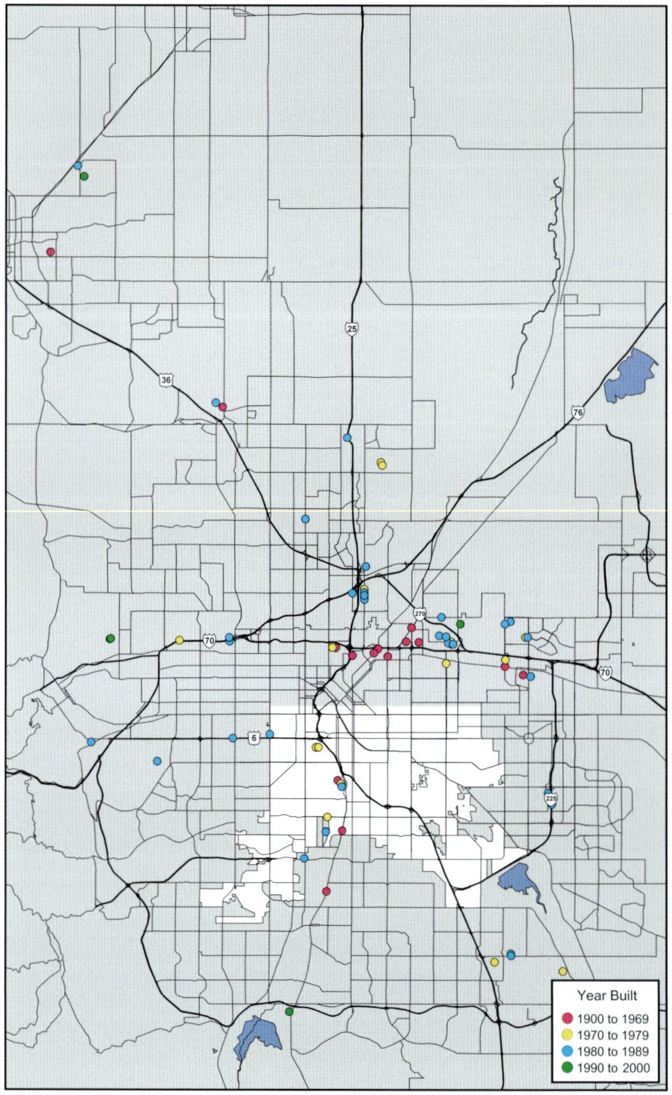

Denver.

FREIGHT FORWARDING

Freight-forwarding facilities have existed for decades, but historically they have not been classified as an independent category of industrial real estate. Their physical characteristics are unique, however, justifying creation of the freight-forwarding primary category. Freight forwarding is an integral function in supply chain management. Of the four major modes of freight transport—airplane, truck, train, and boat—only truck transport directly connects industrial buildings with other real estate sectors, such as retail. *Intermodal freight forwarding,* or the movement of goods from one transport type to another, occurs between airplanes and trucks, trains and trucks, boats and trains, and boats and trucks. *Intramodal transport,* or the movement of goods within the same type of transport, also exists.

Most freight forwarding does not involve the use of buildings. For example, rail yards provide an increasingly common method of transport in major hubs. At such facilities, large magnets attach to individual containers and transfer them onto trucks. This process takes place outside, without buildings. Freight forwarding at harbors, which involves boats and rail or trucks, generally does not require buildings either. This practice does not eliminate the need for ancillary physical structures such as office, warehouse distribution, and manufacturing buildings at freight-forwarding facilities. The two freight-forwarding processes that require buildings are trucks to trucks, an intramodal process, and airplanes to trucks, an intermodal process.

Loading capabilities, building configuration, and space buildout are the physical attributes that classify buildings within the freight-forwarding category. Like heavy distribution buildings, freight-forwarding buildings have docks on two walls. This cross-dock configuration is necessary for the efficient flow-through of freight. The ratio of square feet to docks is very low. Sufficient trailer parking is also a core requirement.

Building configuration is important in the freight-forwarding process. The distance that freight travels from one side of the building to the other is minimized. Therefore, freight-forwarding buildings are rectangular: always longer than deeper.

The internal space buildout of freight-forwarding buildings differs significantly from that of other industrial real estate. Office and warehouse space is minimal; manufacturing space is not present. Because the sole function of freight-forwarding facilities is to move freight through—not to warehouse—these facilities do not have a storage component. The majority of space in freight-forwarding buildings is dedicated to sorting.

Transport by truck and transport by air use two unique building configurations. These buildings are classified as truck terminal and air cargo, respectively. Both have the core differentiating features associated with the freight-forwarding primary category: high loading capabilities, rectangular building configuration, and simple space buildout.

FREIGHT FORWARDING

	SIZE (SQUARE FEET)	PERCENTAGE OFFICE	PERCENTAGE MANFACTURING	CEILING HEIGHT	DOCK RATIO	TRAILER PARKING	PERCENTAGE SITE COVERAGE
TRUCK TERMINAL All truck terminals are cross-docked with a very low square-footage-to-dock ratio: 500 to 1,000 square feet per dock for most buildings. They are rectangular in shape, with an ideal width of approximately 60 feet. Additional differentiating features of truck terminals are low car parking ratio, low ceilings, minimal racking, trailer parking, low site coverage, simple buildout, lack of manufacturing space, and minimal office space.	Up to 100,000	5%	0%	12'–16'	1: 500	Ideally 1 per dock	20%
AIR CARGO Air cargo buildings can be identified by their location: the facilities are located on airport grounds. The function of these facilities is to transfer freight from an airplane onto a truck, or from a truck onto an airplane. A typical air cargo facility is cross-docked. Because this building type is not a warehouse, most space is dedicated to sorting and packaging rather than to storage.	Up to 100,000	10%	0%	Up to 30'	1: 5,000	Frequent	N/A

TRUCK TERMINAL

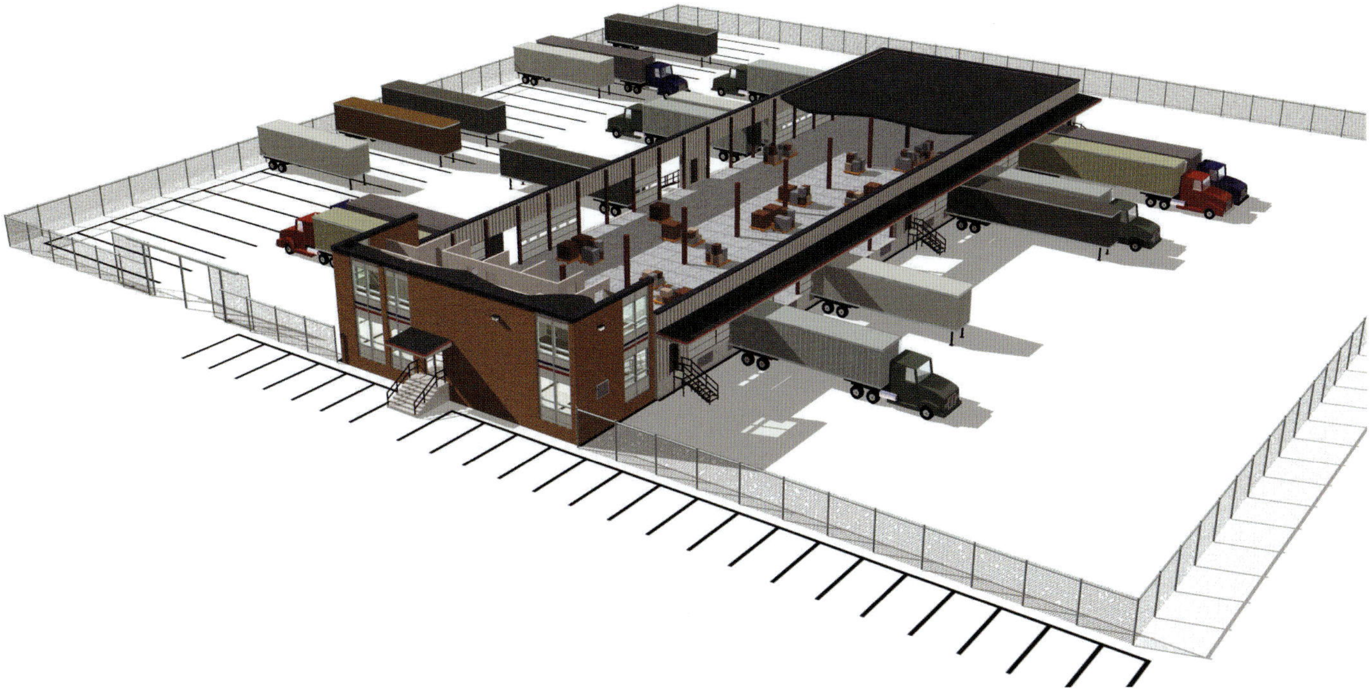

Truck terminals differ significantly from all other types of industrial buildings, although they do have certain exterior features in common with warehouse distribution facilities—specifically, those associated with a distribution function.

All truck terminals are cross-docked with a very low ratio of square feet to docks: 500 to 1,000 square feet per dock for most buildings. Building dimensions are another classification variable. Truck terminals are rectangular, with an ideal depth of approximately 60 feet. In addition to loading and dimensions, the other differentiating features of truck terminals are low car-parking ratio, low ceilings, minimal racking, trailer parking, low site coverage, simple interior buildout, lack of manufacturing space, and minimal office space.

FREIGHT FORWARDING

TRUCK TERMINAL/ EXTERIOR

Truck terminals are small, generally not exceeding 100,000 square feet. Their loading capability is an integral characteristic. In addition to their cross-dock configuration, the large number of docks is unprecedented among other industrial facility types. A ratio of 500 square feet per dock is common, which is warranted by the typical building depth of 60 feet. This requirement is more specific than that imposed on heavy distribution buildings since docks are always along the two longer parallel walls. Truck terminals also require trailer parking. The number of trailer slots ideally should match the number of docks per building.

Automobile parking is not an important feature of truck terminals. One parking space for every 1,500 square feet of building space is sufficient. Truck courts on both sides of the building and heavy trailer parking are the variables that result in a very low site-coverage ratio, which averages around 20 percent.

FREIGHT FORWARDING

TRUCK TERMINAL/ INTERIOR

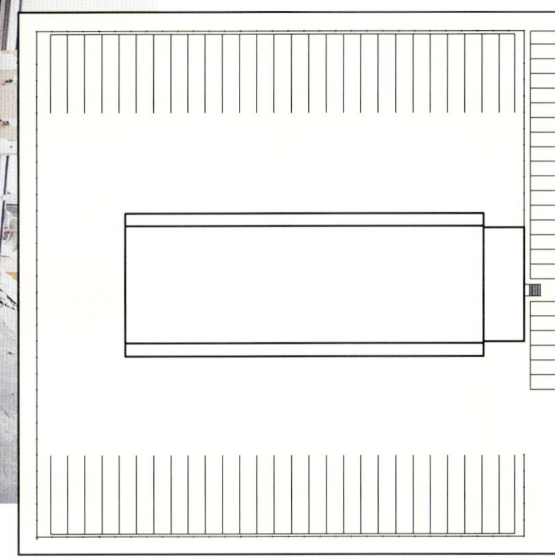

"Terminal" refers to the facility's interior features. Unlike heavy distribution buildings, truck terminals do not warehouse goods. Their sole function is to transfer goods from one truck to another. Because of this function, truck terminals are long and narrow in design.

Because truck terminals transfer rather than store cargo, the facilities have low ceiling heights that range from 12 to 16 feet, which is below the height of any facilities within the warehouse distribution category. Space buildout is very simple. Approximately 95 percent of the building is dedicated to cargo transfer and the remainder is allocated to office space. In some truck terminals, the office, which is situated at the end of the building, can be two stories. In a two-story configuration, the total percentage of office is approximately 10 percent. There is no manufacturing or production space in truck terminals.

Truck terminals have minimal power and floor-load requirements, unlike most industrial building types. Light power is sufficient because no heavy machinery is required to transfer cargo. Smaller buildings operate with a minimum of 200 amperes; larger facilities require no more than 800 amperes. Because of the low ceilings, minimal racking, and lack of heavy machinery, floor thickness does not need to exceed four inches.

FREIGHT FORWARDING

TRUCK TERMINAL/ EVOLUTION

Because truck terminals forward freight, their most common tenants are logistics companies. The accompanying map identifies 16 truck terminals in the Chicago market. Similarly small samples were identified in other metropolitan markets. Because of the small sample size, it is not possible to generalize about the average age and evolutionary pattern for truck terminals.

Truck terminals face the same zoning restrictions as manufacturing facilities. Many municipalities limit, or do not permit, truck terminal use. Any expansion pattern is affected principally by zoning restrictions, followed by variables such as access to highways.

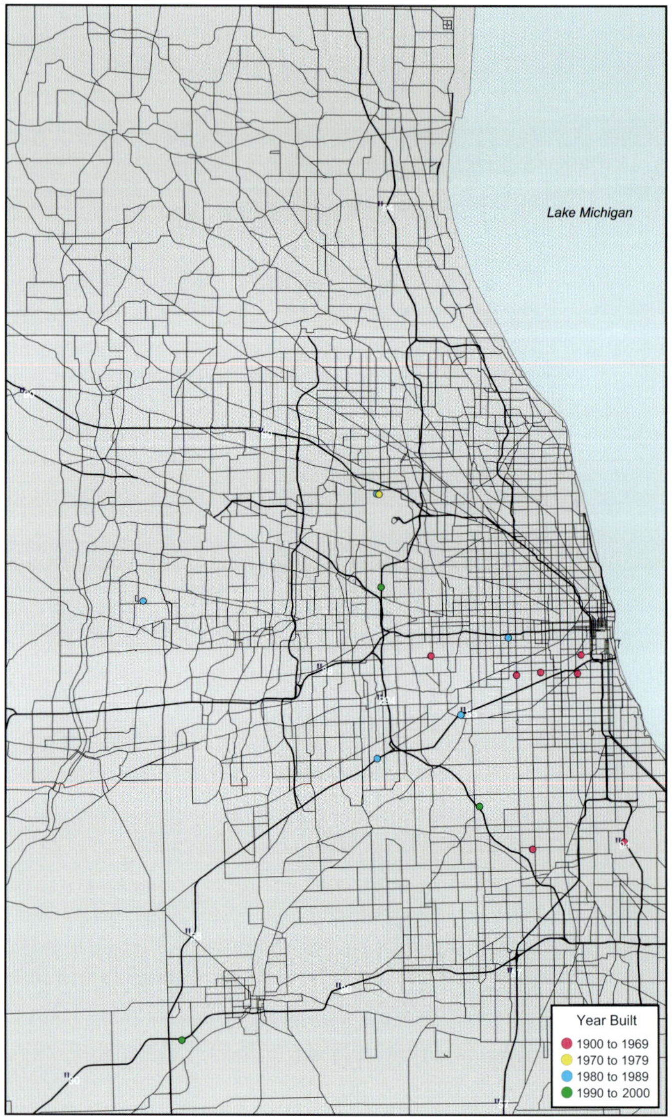

Chicago.

FREIGHT FORWARDING

AIR CARGO

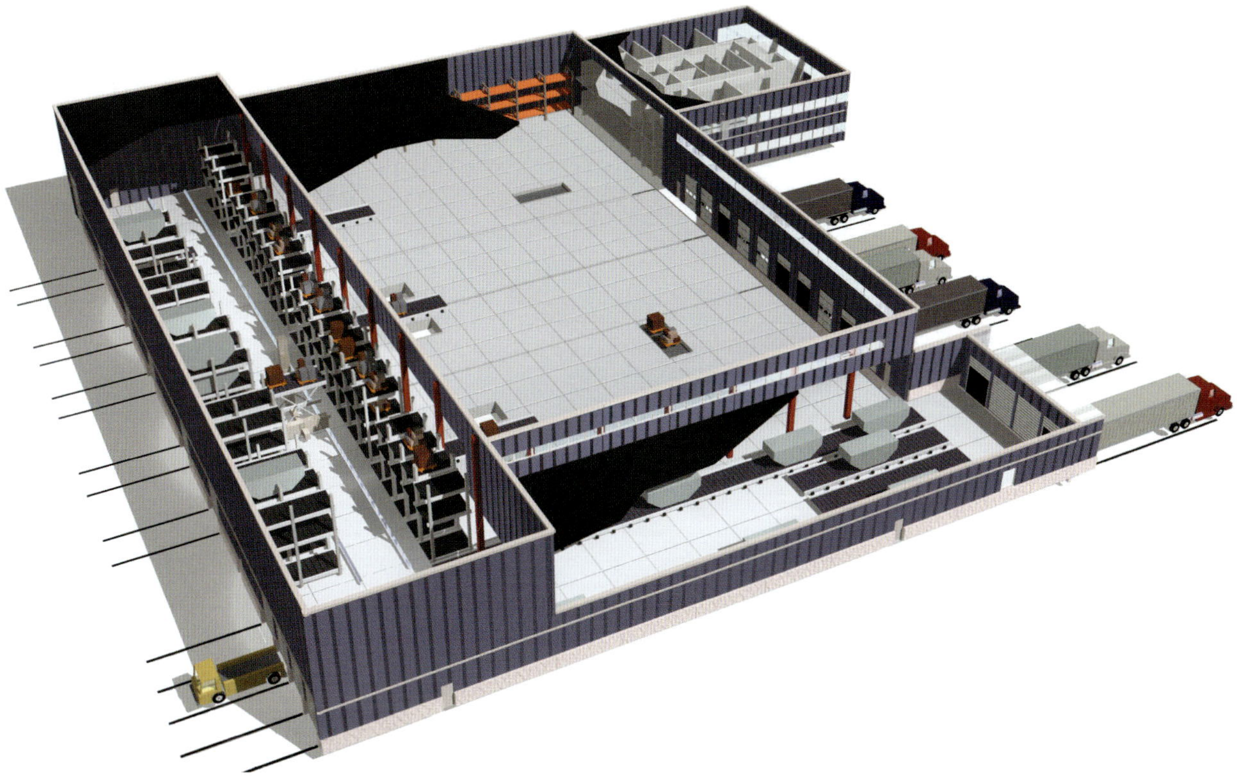

Air cargo buildings can be identified by their location on airport grounds. Their function is to transfer freight from an airplane onto a truck, or from a truck onto an airplane. In order to be classified as air cargo, the transfer must involve an aircraft. Historically, air cargo facilities were associated with a particular type of tenant rather than with physical characteristics—most bulk warehouse or heavy distribution facilities that are used by an airline are commonly referred to as air cargo. However, because the classification process in this guide uses physical characteristics, most of those buildings are classified as warehouse distribution facilities.

The location and freight-handling requirements of these facilities create additional unique characteristics. A typical air cargo facility is cross-docked, which allows ease in the flow-through of cargo. Because this building type is not a warehouse, it has a unique interior buildout, similar to that of truck terminals. Most space is dedicated to sorting and packaging rather than to storage. And because the buildings are located on airport grounds, there are no typical site-coverage ranges.

FREIGHT FORWARDING

AIR CARGO/ EXTERIOR

The exterior of air cargo facilities is influenced by their location on airport property. An entire building can be located behind an airport fence, or the building can straddle the boundary. Air cargo buildings are cross-docked, with standard heavy trucks on the outside and smaller airport-type vehicles that use drive-in doors on the inside. Airplanes pull close to these buildings but do not connect directly as they do at passenger terminals.

Air cargo buildings cover an insignificant portion of space on airport grounds. There is no car parking because of airport security. Parked trailers surround air cargo buildings but do not affect the size of the site. These combined location requirements make site-coverage calculation meaningless.

The size of an air cargo building depends on the volume of freight that an airline transports. Therefore, air cargo buildings are constructed specifically for a tenant's size. In general, the facilities are large, similar to heavy distribution buildings.

AIR CARGO/ INTERIOR

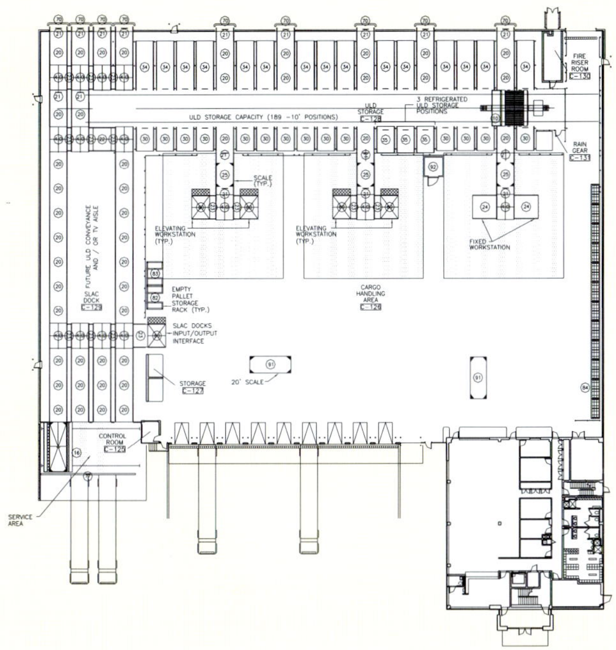

EQUIPMENT DESCRIPTION	ITEM #
ELEVATING TRANSFER VEHICLE (ETV)	ITEM 10
TRAVELING TRUCK DOCK	ITEM 16
POWERED DECK, 10' NARROW EDGE LEADING (NEL)	ITEM 20
POWERED DECK, INTERFACE, NARROW EDGE LEADING (NEL)	ITEM 21
POWERED DECK, 10' WIDE EDGE LEADING (WEL)	ITEM 22
POWERED DECK, INTERFACE, WIDE EDGE LEADING (WEL)	ITEM 23
FIXED HEIGHT WORKSTATION, (WEL)	ITEM 24
POWERED DECK,10' NEL, WITH BUILT-IN SCALE	ITEM 25
PORTABLE WORKSTATION, (10')	ITEM 26
FRICTION POWERED STORAGE DECK, 10' (NEL)	ITEM 30
FRICTION POWERED STORAGE DECK, 20' (NEL)	ITEM 34
REFRIGERATED STORAGE DECK, 10' (NEL)	ITEM 35
RIGHT ANGLE DECK (RAD), 10'	ITEM 40
ELEVATING WORKSTATION,(WEL)	ITEM 60
RAM PROTECTION, DOLLY / TRANSPORTER (NEL)	ITEM 70
RAM PROTECTION,ELEVATING WORKSTATION (10'+ INTERFACE)	ITEM 73
RAM PROTECTION, FIXED HEIGHT WORKSTATION	ITEM 74
RAM PROTECTION, TRUCK TRANSFER	ITEM 77
RACK STRUCTURE, ETV SYSTEM	ITEM 81
EMPTY PALLET RACK, 88"	ITEM 82
EMPTY PALLET RACK, 96"	ITEM 83
BULK CARGO RACK	ITEM 84
FLOOR SCALE, 20'	ITEM 91
WALK-IN COOLER	ITEM 92

A contemporary air cargo facility consists of four sections: office, sorting and weighing, storage, and cargo flow-through. The office section does not exceed 10 percent of total space and is separated from the cargo area. Mezzanine office and separate office buildouts, which can be two stories, are common. A sorting and weighing section is located along the wall with docks. This area—where transferred cargo is sorted, weighed, and packed—is the largest. The cargo is then placed in a storage area before being loaded onto an airplane. Because air cargo buildings are not warehouses, the storage section accounts for only about 30 percent of the entire building. Cargo that arrives packed in containers moves through a fourth area, where it is immediately transferred between trucks and planes.

The freight-forwarding process is primarily automated, especially in more contemporary facilities, requiring few workers. Freight-forwarding equipment includes multiple powered decks, scales, elevating workstations and transfer vehicles, as well as multiple friction-powered storage decks.

The ceiling heights of air cargo buildings vary. A building can have a different ceiling height in each of its four sections. In general, air cargo buildings have ceiling heights of about 24 feet, which is comparable to warehouse distribution buildings.

FREIGHT FORWARDING

AIR CARGO/ EVOLUTION

Air cargo buildings exhibit the same evolutionary pattern as airport hangars. Both are entirely dependent on the presence of airports. Advances in the field of logistics are affecting the physical evolutionary pattern of this facility type. The trend toward increased automation in contemporary air cargo buildings is resulting in fewer employees per square foot and this trend is likely to continue.

In recent years, a hybrid form of this property type has emerged that is a cross between a heavy distribution and an air cargo building. In fact, physically it is a cross-docked heavy distribution building with dock doors on one side and air cargo–type drive-in doors on the opposite side. These buildings are large, with accompanying high ceilings. Compared to pure freight-forwarding and warehouse distribution buildings, these hybrids are few in number; however, new ones are being added. Although this guide does not categorize hybrids because they could fall under either type of property classification, this one falls into the freight-forwarding primary and air cargo secondary categories.

DATA SWITCH CENTER

Data switch center is the newest category of industrial real estate. In the past, this type of facility sometimes has been classified within the office sector or not classified at all. Data switch centers generally were not considered investment properties and, in most cases, were owner-occupied. Although many remain owner-occupied, in recent years they have become investment opportunities.

Data switch centers are created either through new construction or by conversion of existing properties. No specific type of building is converted to data switch center use—office, loft, and industrial buildings are all likely to be converted if they meet a specified set of requirements, the most important of which is access to fiber optic cable.

The physical characteristics of all data switch centers, whether converted from other buildings or newly constructed, are most consistent with the industrial sector of real estate. Core differentiating features are power and floor-load requirements. With a minimum power requirement of 60 watts per square foot, data switch centers have the highest power requirement of all industrial building types. Most data switch center tenants anticipate needing up to 200 watts per square foot in the future. A high floor load per square foot is required because the equipment that is commonly stored and operated in data switch centers is both heavy and compact.

An additional important and unique variable is system redundancy, or backup. A data switch center needs to remain in operation without interruption. All heating, ventilation, and air conditioning (HVAC); electrical; and fire-suppression systems, therefore, have backup systems.

DATA SWITCH CENTER

	SIZE	PERCENTAGE OFFICE	PERCENTAGE MANFACTURING	CEILING HEIGHT	DOCK RATIO	POWER	FIRE SUPPRESSION
DATA SWITCH CENTER Data switch centers can be redeveloped from older properties or constructed as new high-tech buildings. Redeveloped properties have a wide variety of sizes and configurations and are difficult to identify from the exterior. New high-tech buildings are more uniform and can be identified more readily. The core differentiating variables are high floor load, heavy power, and redundancy of all power, security, and fire detection and suppression systems.	Any	1%	0%	14' +	0 in most buildings	60 to 200 Watts psf, redundant	Gas-based with early detection and backup

DATA SWITCH CENTER

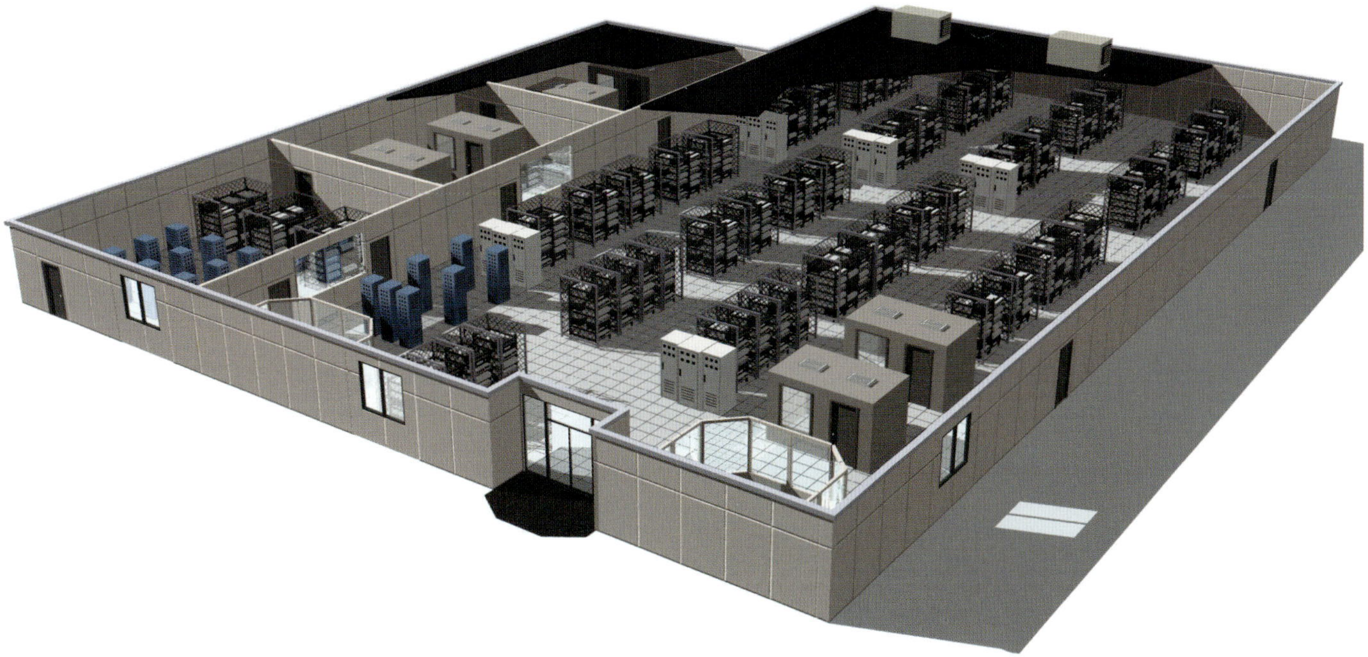

DATA SWITCH CENTER

Data switch centers can be redeveloped from older properties or constructed as new high-tech buildings. Redeveloped properties have a wide variety of sizes and configurations and are, therefore, difficult to identify from the exterior. New high-tech buildings are more uniform and can be identified more readily.

The prominent interior characteristics of data switch centers clearly identify them from the interior by the equipment used and the level of security present. Additional interior core variables are high floor load and heavy power resources. Redundancy of all power, security, and fire-detection and suppression systems is required. Such a high level of system redundancy is not found in any other industrial category. Unique exterior features include site coverage, site security, and loading. Building size and number of stories vary too much to be a factor in classification.

DATA SWITCH CENTER

DATA SWITCH CENTER/ EXTERIOR

Data switch centers do not have a specific size range and can be single story or multistory. Certain exterior characteristics, however, differentiate data switch centers from other industrial categories. They do not have loading requirements; either they lack existing dock doors, or the dock doors have been sealed. To maximize building dryness and security, data switch centers require minimal wall and roof penetrations.

Security is a site requirement and a unique core variable of data switch centers. Stand-alone facilities are usually fenced, with monitored campus gates and video surveillance of the grounds. Only a few R&D flex buildings have a similarly high security requirement.

Average site-coverage ratio is another core feature differentiating data switch centers. The facilities have very few employees and infrequent visitors. The car-parking ratio, therefore, is low: on average, one space for every 2,000 square feet. The low parking ratio, coupled with the absence of truck courts, results in a site-coverage ratio as high as 60-plus percent.

A final exterior feature is a utility area that houses power generators and other support systems for HVAC, fire suppression, and security.

DATA SWITCH CENTER

DATA SWITCH CENTER/ INTERIOR

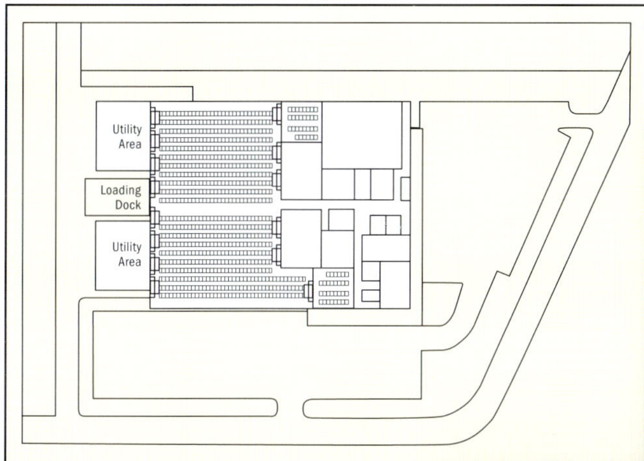

The interior features of data switch centers differ significantly from those of other industrial facilities. However, the attributes of power and floor load align this category with the rest of the industrial sector. Extremely high power, ranging from 60 to 200 watts per square foot, is required to operate data switch centers. A 50,000-square-foot data switch center would need 6,250 amperes at 480 volts in order to meet this requirement. Heavy manufacturing buildings have amperage that reaches those levels, but not at the per-square-foot basis. Data switch centers also need backup generators, preferably fed from dual power sources from two separate grids.

Data switch centers have raised floors. Because of the weight of the equipment, high floor-load capacity is also essential. The minimum floor load is 150 pounds per square foot.

Security is even more pronounced inside these facilities. Security features include surveillance cameras in aisles and at building entrances, motion detectors, biometric access sensors, and specially trained guards.

Fire suppression is a core attribute of data switch centers. Equipment housed in data switch centers is sensitive to water. Therefore, the facilities have gas-based fire-suppression systems with early detection, backup, and dry pipes.

DATA SWITCH CENTER

DATA SWITCH CENTER/ EVOLUTION

Data switch centers are similar to airport hangars and air cargo buildings in that their location depends on an external variable—access to fiber optic cable. Their geographic expansion pattern, therefore, is directly tied to the expansion of fiber optic cable. The need for security also affects geographic pattern; the specific location of these facilities is typically not advertised. Because the design, size, and configuration of these buildings are heavily influenced by technological advances, this property type is expected to undergo the most changes in the future.

LOCATION

OVERVIEW

In this guide, six primary and 12 secondary categories of industrial real estate have been classified according to specific physical characteristics. The purpose of this section is to identify variables that affect geographic location of industrial facilities, specifically whether buildings with consistent physical characteristics also have similar geographic attributes. The following nine industrial categories—eight secondary categories and the multitenant primary category—were selected for this analysis:

- Warehouse distribution primary category
  - Regional warehouse
  - Bulk warehouse
  - Heavy distribution
- Manufacturing primary category
  - Light manufacturing
  - Heavy manufacturing
- Flex primary category
  - R&D flex
  - Office showroom
- Multitenant primary category
- Freight-forwarding primary category
  - Truck terminal

The air cargo, airport hangar, rack-supported warehouse, and refrigerated distribution secondary categories and data switch center primary category were not analyzed because sample size was insufficient or because their location depends on a single variable. Airport hangars and air cargo buildings have consistent locations in all markets; they are located on airport grounds. Data switch centers require access to fiber optic cable, which restricts their locations. Limited sample sizes of rack-supported and refrigerated distribution buildings eliminated them from the analysis. Both those types of buildings, however, belong to the warehouse distribution primary category, making access to highways a primary determinant of location.

A wide variety of factors affect location of industrial properties. The factors discussed in this section include zoning, access to transportation infrastructure, land availability and price, and proximity to a labor pool. Their influence varies across primary property types, depending on both the building's physical characteristics and its use.

ZONING

Industrial uses have historically been relegated to the least desirable areas of cities, but in recent decades—as a result of efforts to encourage and retain an industrial employment base—communities have paid greater attention to reserving adequate land for industrial purposes. Zoning regulations play a crucial role in determining where industrial uses are located, and the degree of influence is proportional to the desirability of the building type to residential communities. Manufacturing buildings provoke the strongest negative reaction from communities and, as a result, they face the strongest development restrictions. Flex buildings encounter the fewest restrictions and may be located even in high-income areas.

OVERVIEW

ACCESS TO TRANSPORTATION INFRASTRUCTURE

Access to transportation infrastructure is fundamental to all types of industrial properties, although requirements vary by category. Today, most distribution relies on trucking, so proximity to major highways is key for warehouse distribution buildings and truck terminals. Railroads, which are less likely to be used to fulfill warehouse and distribution functions, are used more extensively for manufacturing operations and can influence site selection for manufacturing facilities, especially heavy manufacturing plants. Airports also exert a strong attraction for industrial uses. This "airport effect" is the result not only of the need for facilities to serve air cargo but also of other factors common in areas surrounding airports: good highway access, available and inexpensive land, and favorable zoning. Access to infrastructure plays a lesser role for R&D flex and multitenant property types because of their lesser dependence on any form of transportation.

LAND AVAILABILITY AND PRICE

Industrial buildings are typically single-story structures that require large land areas to accommodate on-site loading, truck turn-around areas, and trailer and automobile parking in addition to the building. The scarcity of large-scale developable sites has meant that many low-density industrial developments have fanned farther out from city centers. Cost of land is also a factor. With the exception of R&D flex and data switch centers, industrial developments are price-sensitive because of their lower rental rates relative to other types of commercial development.

PROXIMITY TO LABOR

Proximity to an employee base is another factor affecting industrial location, especially for labor-intensive uses accommodated by manufacturing and flex buildings. This relationship is less pronounced in warehouse distribution, freight forwarding, and multitenant buildings, which are characterized by relatively low ratios of employees to square feet of space.

FUTURE TRENDS

Changes in supply chain management are affecting the location of industrial properties. The "need for speed" in distribution, particularly of high-value goods, has made proximity to major highways and airports more important than ever. There is also a growing trend to consolidate regional distribution networks into large-scale "mega" distribution centers. These types of facilities have huge land requirements, while still requiring access to labor and transportation networks. Another factor is co-location, which results from manufacturing and logistics collaboration. Often, suppliers will locate near their customers to take advantage of synergies and transportation cost savings.

Redevelopment is another trend to watch. As greenfield sites on the edges of metropolitan areas become more scarce and expensive, growing attention is being given to the reuse of urban infill and brownfield sites for industrial uses. Some cities provide incentives such as tax increment financing and funds for environmental remediation to encourage redevelopment of such sites.

OVERVIEW

METHODOLOGY

This section provides an overview of the location characteristics of industrial properties throughout the United States, with a focus on the major markets of Atlanta, Chicago, Dallas/Fort Worth, Denver, and Los Angeles. Using the CoStar Property database, a sample was identified for each selected property type in the five cities. Because this guide identifies new property types not used by CoStar Property, individual buildings in the database were reclassified utilizing user-defined fields. Only the buildings with sufficient information were considered. The resulting samples are random in terms of location, since only physical characteristics were used in this process.

Samples were overlaid with demographic variables using MapInfo. The four demographic ranges on each map, depicted by four different shades of the same color, were generated by MapInfo's demographic component using 1999 census data on a zip-code level and the natural break algorithm. This algorithm minimizes the difference between data values and the average value per range. This approach does not generate equal ranges but gives a truer representation of the entire population.

The demographic variables analyzed are blue-collar workers, average household income and total retail spending. The blue-collar data represent labor markets. Average household income is used as a proxy for land prices, which are not generally available on a consistent basis for multiple markets. Land in high-income areas is assumed to be more expensive than land in low-income areas. Total retail spending was considered as a factor only in connection with regional warehouse and office showroom properties. The former have a direct retail connection, while the latter have a retail space component.

WAREHOUSE DISTRIBUTION

REGIONAL WAREHOUSE

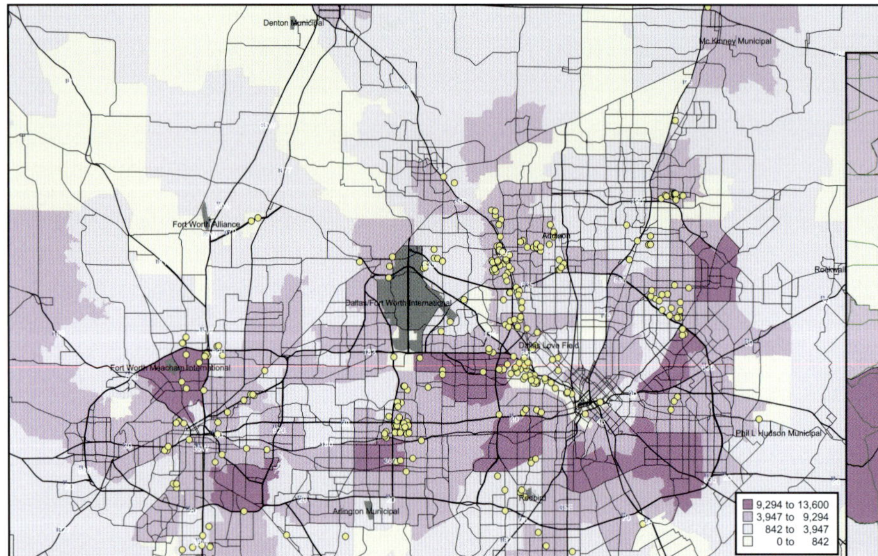

Dallas/Fort Worth.

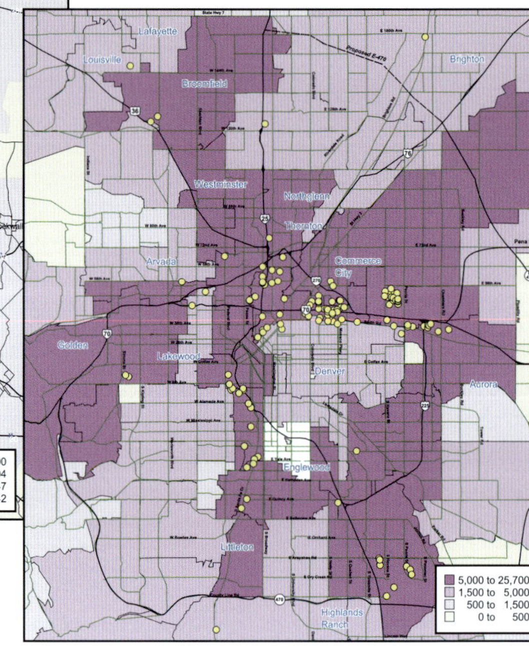

Denver.

Access to highways and airports is an important location determinant for regional warehouses, whose primary function is to store and distribute goods. The typical regional warehouse employee belongs to the blue-collar workforce, so these facilities often locate near areas with high populations of blue-collar workers. Because regional warehouses are often the last step in the supply chain before distribution to retail outlets, there is a relationship between their location, the location of retail facilities, and areas with higher levels of total retail spending.

The accompanying maps identify the locations of regional warehouses in Chicago, Dallas/Fort Worth, and Denver. In Dallas/Fort Worth and Denver, the vast majority of these facilities are located along major highways. In Chicago, however, this relationship is slightly less pronounced, and O'Hare International Airport attracts a large percentage of the area's regional warehouses.

In Denver, more than 90 percent of regional warehouses sampled are located in areas with high concentrations of blue-collar workers. In Dallas/Fort Worth, the location of regional warehouses does not appear to dominate a specific geographic location in relation to blue-collar workers. However, when the year of construction is introduced as a variable, a correlation can be seen between the location of regional warehouses built from 1970 to 2000 in the Dallas metropolitan center and the presence of blue-collar workers. This finding extends to other major industrial real estate markets across the country.

Because regional warehouses directly serve retail outlets, their location is more strongly correlated with retail spending than with income. In Chicago, the strongest concentration of regional warehouses is in areas with high total retail spending, excluding O'Hare International Airport. In contrast, fewer than 10 percent of regional warehouses are located in areas with low retail spending.

In summary, as their physical and functional characteristics suggest, regional warehouses are primarily located in areas with good highway access. However, demographic variables often affect their location as well. Locations where highways intersect areas with high total retail spending, as well as the presence of blue-collar workers, attract more regional warehouses than those that do not share such characteristics.

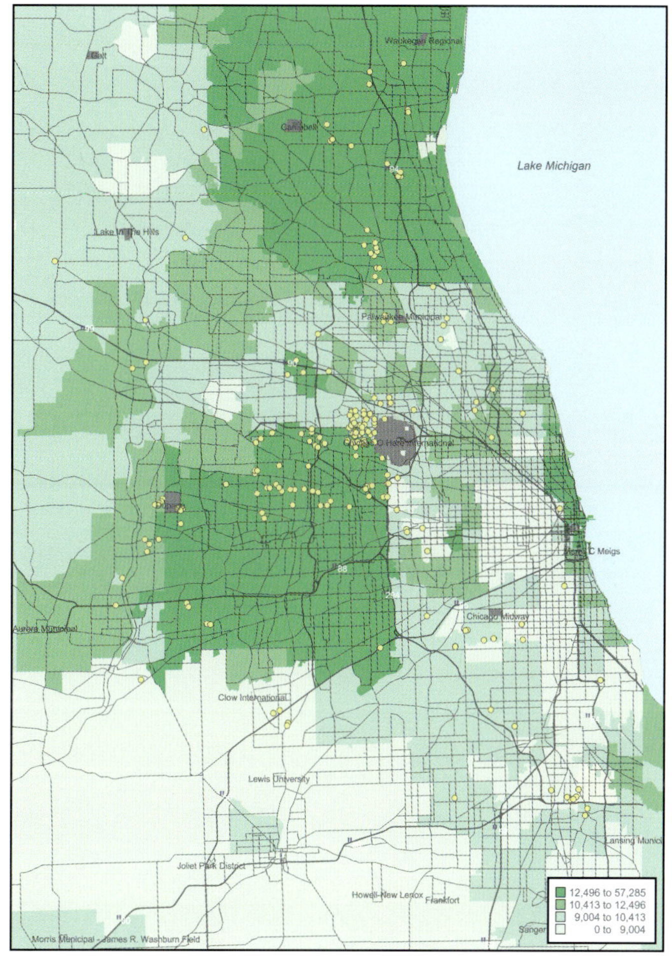

Chicago.

WAREHOUSE DISTRIBUTION

BULK WAREHOUSE

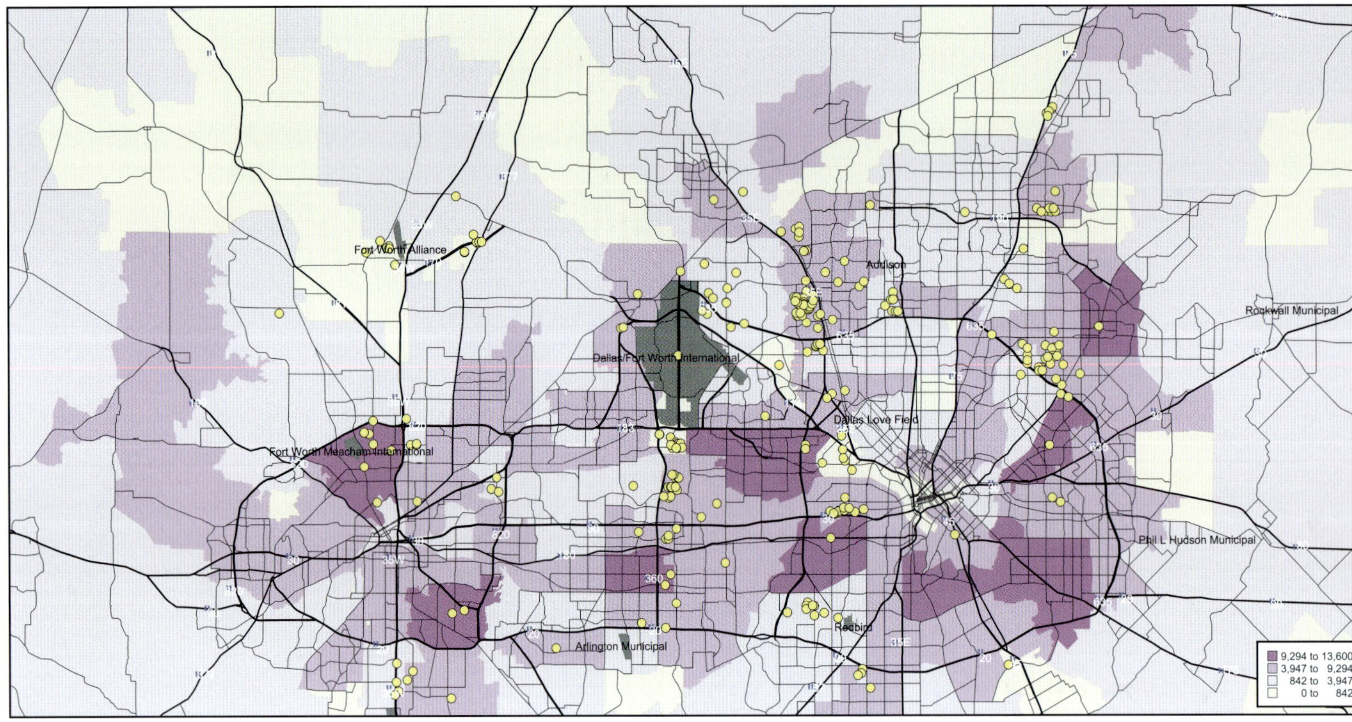

Dallas/Fort Worth.

Bulk warehouses serve functions similar to those of regional warehouses, but the former generally store larger quantities of goods and serve larger geographic regions. In most cases, bulk warehouses rely entirely on trucking for distribution of goods, although rail is sometimes used for goods such as industrial commodities. Therefore, access to highway infrastructure is crucial, while rail is often considered an amenity. Today, more and more companies are consolidating their warehousing operations into a few strategically located, extremely large bulk warehouses. Their larger building size and site requirements have a major impact on their location within metropolitan and regional areas.

As illustrated on the maps of the Atlanta and Dallas/Fort Worth markets, bulk warehouses generally are located in areas near airports and close to major highways. These attributes are consistent across markets and all warehouse distribution secondary categories.

Bulk warehouses demonstrate a low ratio of employees to square feet of space and therefore are not strongly dependent on proximity to blue-collar labor. In Dallas/Fort Worth, a small proportion of bulk warehouses is located in areas with the highest concentration of blue-collar workers, while the majority is in areas with the lowest concentration. This relationship is very different for labor-intensive building types such as light manufacturing and R&D flex.

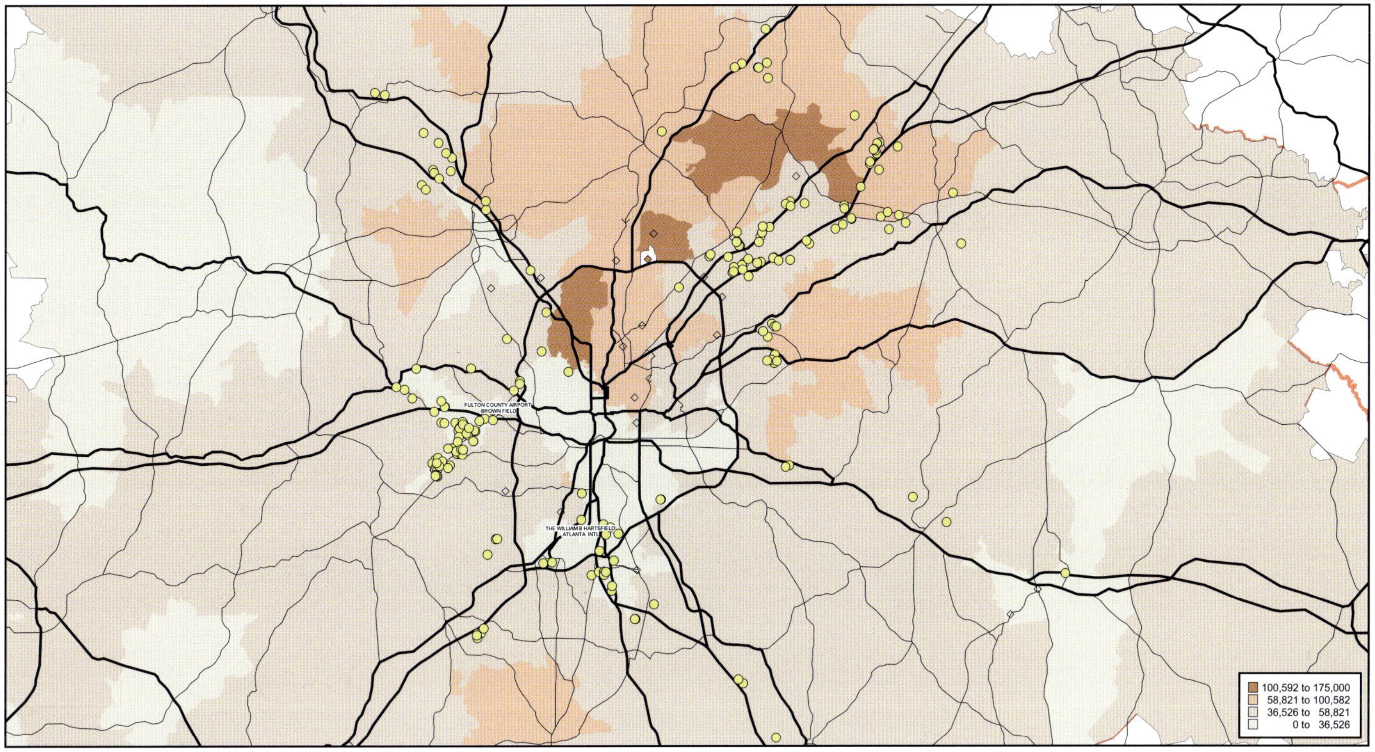

Atlanta.

The accompanying map depicting a sample of more than 200 bulk warehouses in the Atlanta market shows a definitive relationship between the location of these facilities and average household income. As expected, bulk warehouses predominate in low-to-medium-income areas and are seldom found in high-income areas. Two major forces drive this relationship. First, zoning restricts these types of buildings from locating in high-income areas because of their size, appearance, function, and generation of heavy truck traffic. Cost of land also is a factor. The rental rates that can be achieved at bulk warehouses limit the prices that developers can afford to pay for their sites.

In summary, like other secondary categories of the warehouse distribution category, bulk warehouses are generally found along highways and near airports. This relationship is consistent with their function to store and distribute goods. In terms of demographics, average household income is a better indicator of potential location than the presence of a blue-collar workforce.

WAREHOUSE DISTRIBUTION

HEAVY DISTRIBUTION

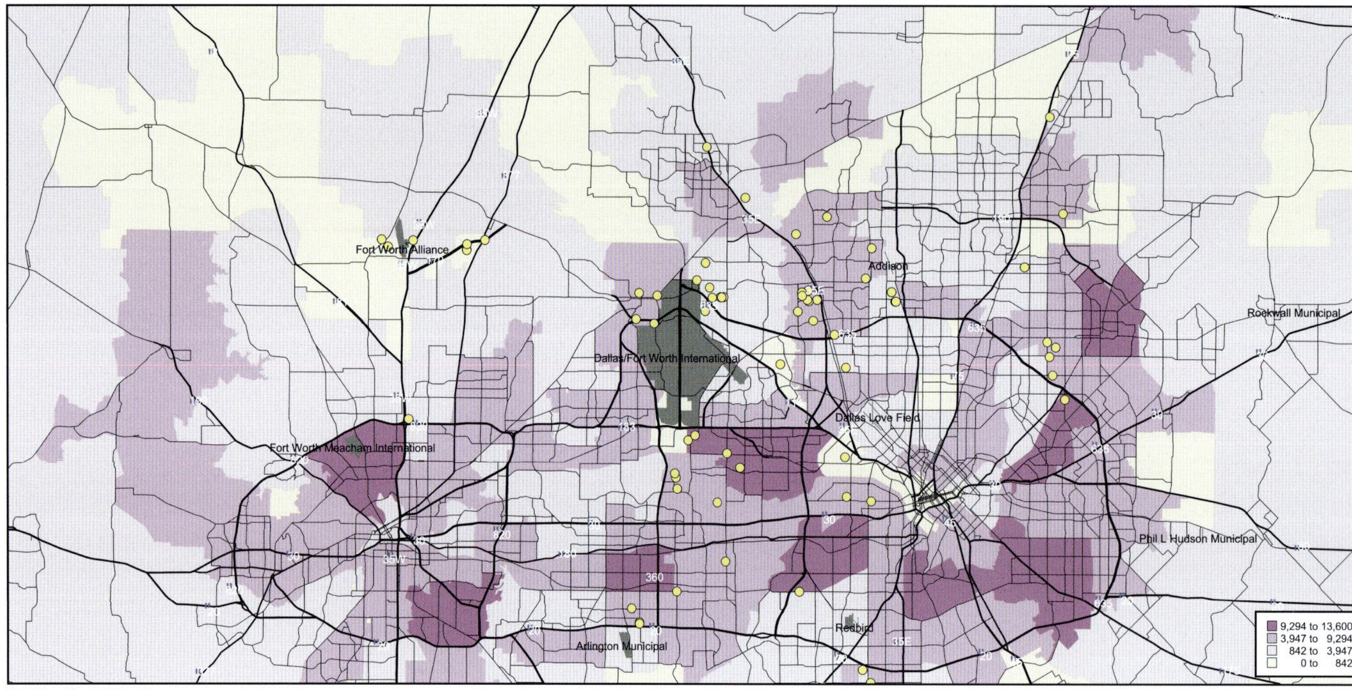

Dallas/Fort Worth.

Heavy distribution buildings, in conformity with their functional requirements, have a cross-dock configuration that is typically suitable only for truck transportation. Therefore, highway infrastructure influences location of these buildings.

The accompanying maps display a sample of heavy distribution buildings in the Chicago and Dallas/Fort Worth markets. Consistent with other buildings in the warehouse distribution category, heavy distribution buildings are located along highways and around airports. The connection to highways in Chicago is less pronounced, possibly because of additional variables such as zoning, demographics, and the cost of land.

In the Dallas/Fort Worth market, the location of heavy distribution buildings is definitively connected to the presence of a blue-collar workforce. As the concentration of these workers increases, so does the number of heavy distribution buildings. This relationship holds for the first three demographic ranges, depicted by the three lightest shades of purple on the map. The relationship between presence of blue-collar workers and location of heavy distribution facilities is stronger than that for bulk warehouses. Other major markets such as Atlanta, Chicago, and Denver display a similar correlation.

Heavy distribution buildings tend to be located in areas of low land prices (using average household income as a proxy). In addition to zoning restrictions and accessibility issues, the cost of land is critical in underwriting new construction. The cost of land in high-income areas is typically too high for most industrial facilities, with the exception of R&D flex and data switch centers. As seen in the Chicago sample, fewer than 10 percent of the area's heavy distribution buildings are located in areas with the highest average household income.

Consistent with the warehouse distribution primary category overall, heavy distribution facilities typically are found along highway corridors and in clusters around airports. However, they are not immune to other factors. Assuming favorable zoning, other variables that influence their location are cost of land and access to blue-collar labor.

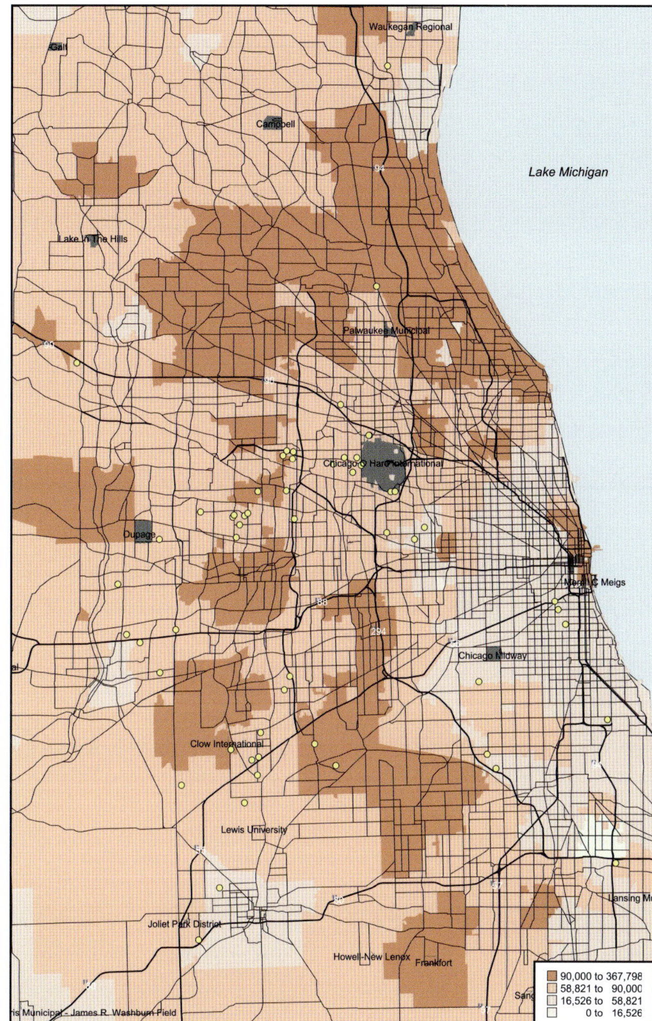

Chicago.

MANUFACTURING

LIGHT MANUFACTURING

The role of light manufacturing buildings is evolving from pure manufacturing and assembly to include warehousing and distribution. Nevertheless, their primary function remains creation of goods, which suggests different location drivers for these types of buildings than for warehouse distribution buildings.

The accompanying maps show approximately 300 light manufacturing buildings in Chicago and 400 properties in the Los Angeles market. In both markets, the locations of these buildings are not confined to highways. Instead, zoning is a primary location factor. When an area is zoned for manufacturing use, multiple manufacturing facilities are constructed near each other. Thus, zoning restrictions result in a clustering effect that is noticeable in both cities.

Unlike warehouse distribution buildings, light manufacturing facilities typically employ a high number of workers per square foot; therefore, access to labor is an important location variable for this facility type. As the Chicago map shows, a high concentration of light manufacturing facilities exists in areas with the highest blue-collar worker population, and no light manufacturing buildings are located in areas with the lowest number of blue-collar workers. This relationship occurs in other major markets across the United States, confirming proximity to labor as a meaningful driver behind the location of light manufacturing buildings.

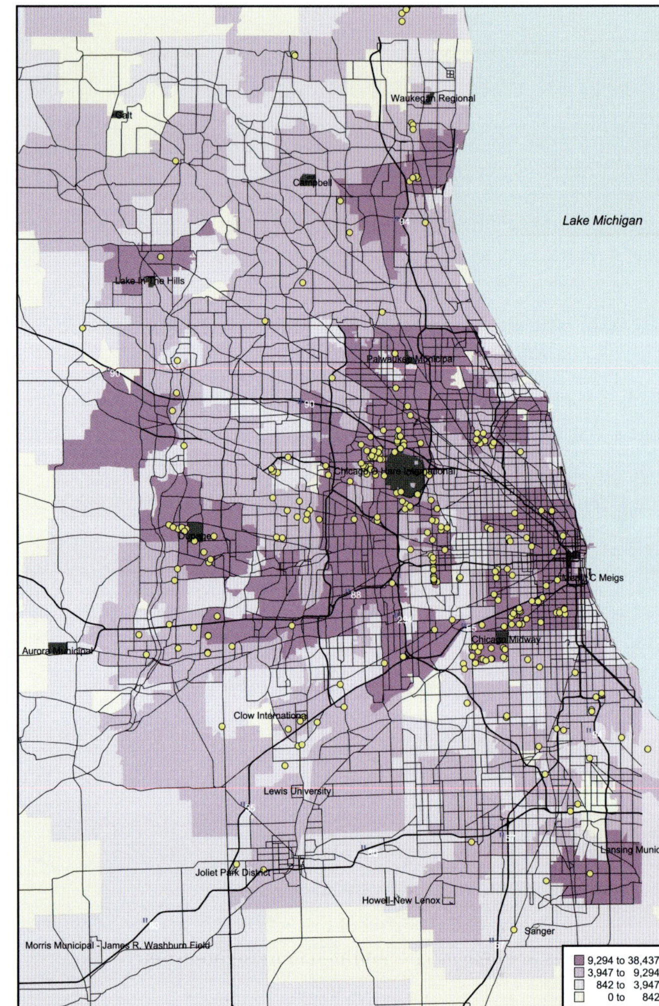

Chicago.

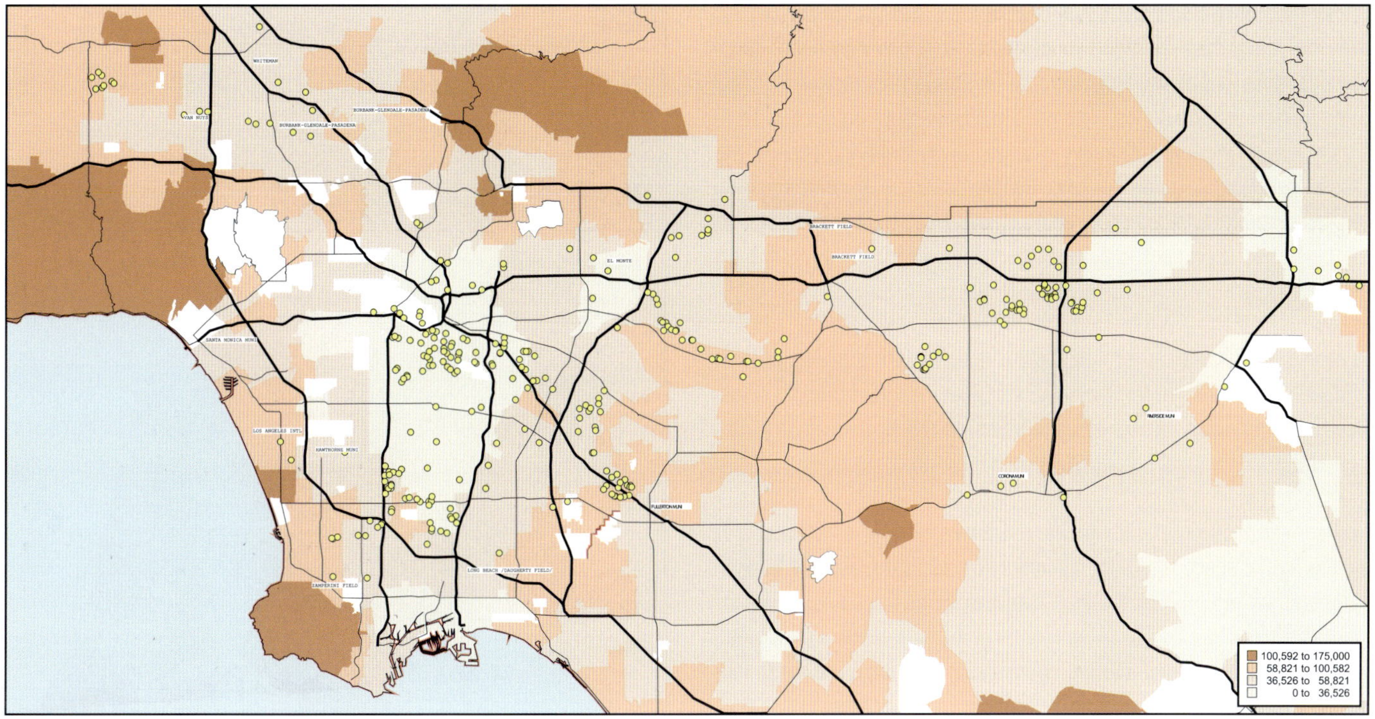

Los Angeles.

As is the case for warehouse distribution facilities, an inverse relationship exists between location of light manufacturing buildings and average household income. As the Los Angeles map illustrates, no light manufacturing facilities are present in areas with the highest average household income, and only a few exist in the second-highest range. Rather, these facilities are heavily concentrated in those areas representing the two lowest income ranges (approximately 80 percent of the sample). This pattern is consistent in other major U.S. markets. The link between building location and income is stronger for light manufacturing facilities than for warehouse distribution buildings. The high cost of land and zoning restrictions prevent manufacturing development in higher-income areas.

In summary, light manufacturing buildings cluster in appropriately zoned areas. Because their primary function is production instead of distribution, their location is not strongly dependent on highway access. Instead, access to labor is a more important factor. Finally, they do not locate in high-income areas, regardless of zoning, because of prohibitive land costs.

MANUFACTURING

HEAVY MANUFACTURING

Heavy manufacturing buildings are even more geographically limited than their light manufacturing counterparts. Because they house functions as industrial as the processing of raw materials, zoning is on top of the list of location drivers. The accompanying maps depict two samples of approximately 100 heavy manufacturing buildings each in the Chicago and Los Angeles markets. Comparing these maps to those in the light manufacturing section, an overlap of location is evident in both markets. This alignment is a result of zoning, which drives both light and heavy manufacturing buildings to locate in clusters.

Access to rail is critical for many heavy manufacturing buildings. This requirement is stronger for heavy than for light manufacturing facilities. Access to highways, a core variable affecting the warehouse distribution and truck terminal categories, is of secondary importance.

Heavy manufacturing buildings have a lower ratio of employees per square foot of space than light manufacturing facilities, especially when compared to assembly buildings. Nevertheless, as the Chicago map indicates, the connection between presence of blue-collar workers and location of heavy manufacturing buildings is noticeable. This relationship is even more pronounced in other major U.S. markets.

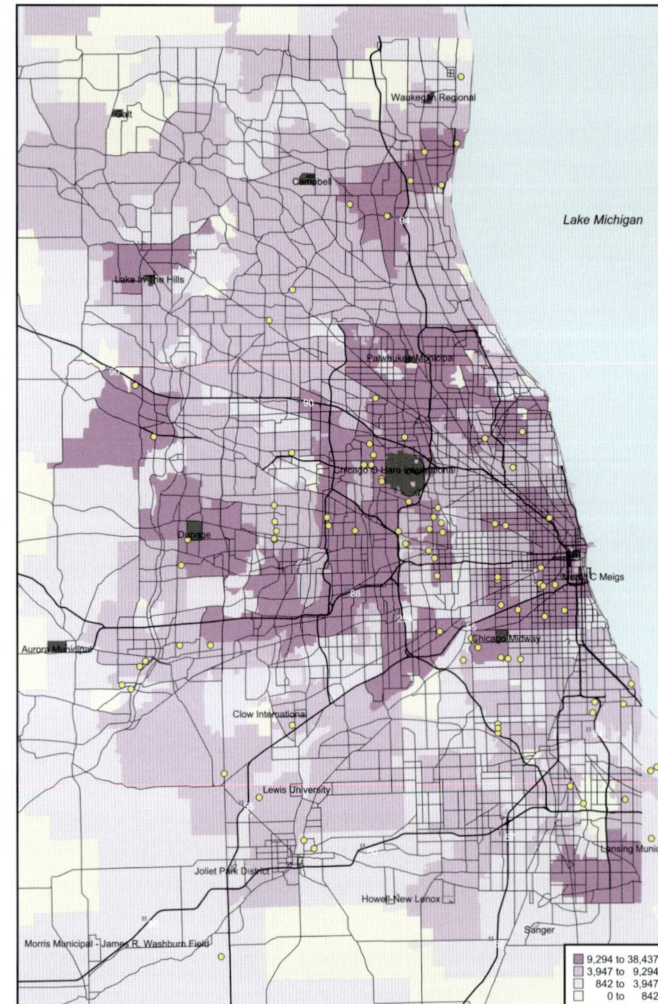

Chicago.

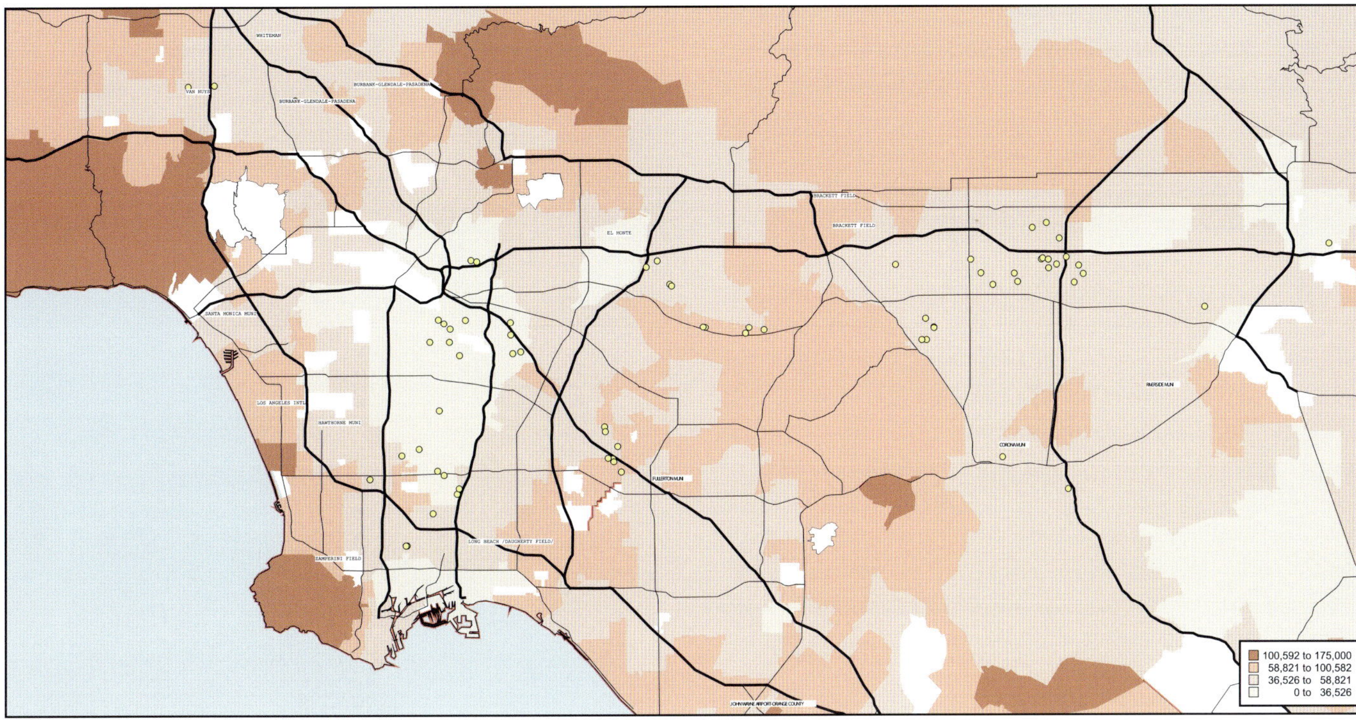

Los Angeles.

The relationship between location and average household income is clearly defined for heavy manufacturing buildings. As the Los Angeles map shows, the dominant concentration of these types of buildings is in the areas of lowest income. It is the buildings' appearance and function, more than cost of land, that make them undesirable in most areas, resulting in restrictive zoning and limited location choices.

In summary, heavy manufacturing buildings perform functions that make them undesirable in most areas; therefore, zoning heavily determines their location. After zoning, access to labor and rail are the two most important determinants of location.

FLEX

R&D FLEX

R&D flex buildings are the least industrial of all industrial building types. They generally house office, laboratory, and high-tech light manufacturing functions that involve minimal truck loading. Zoning for these facilities is less restrictive and, therefore, other factors such as visibility, access to major streets, and demographics influence their location. The two accompanying maps depict a sample of 160 R&D flex buildings in the Chicago market.

R&D flex facilities typically engage a high number of workers per square foot of space, which is reflected in their high car-parking requirement. These facilities therefore require proximity to areas with a high concentration of blue-collar workers. In the Chicago sample, most R&D flex facilities are located in areas with the highest proportion of blue-collar workers. Moreover, no R&D flex buildings are present in areas with a low incidence of blue-collar workers. This finding is consistent in other major U.S. industrial markets, with the exception of Dallas/Fort Worth, which has older R&D flex facilities situated in areas with a small blue-collar workforce. However, when focusing only on buildings built within the last 20 years in Dallas/Fort Worth, the relationship strengthens.

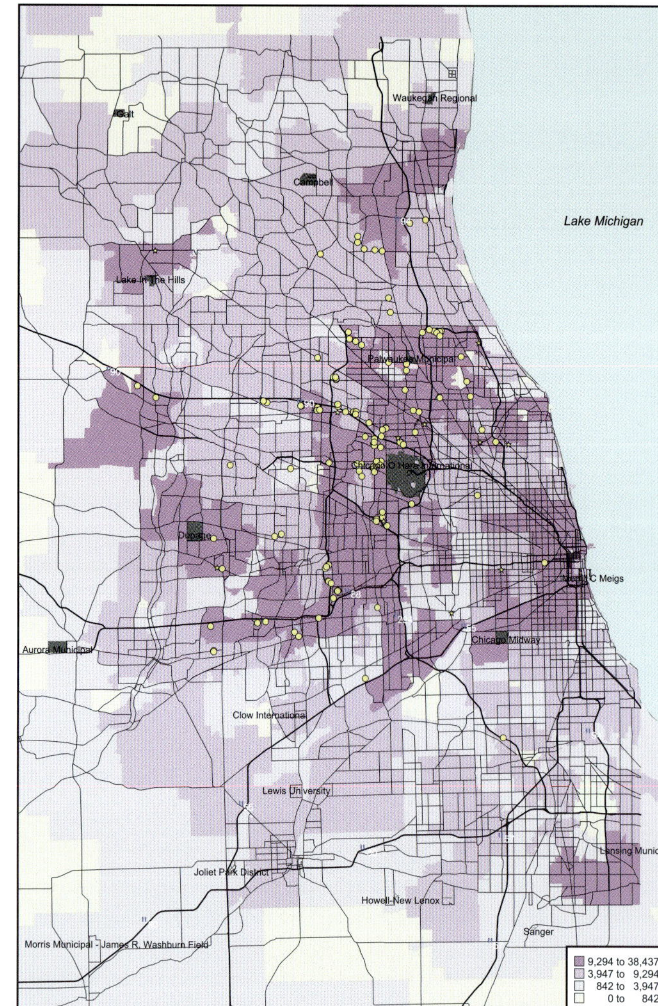

Chicago.

The high cost of land in higher-income areas makes development of most industrial real estate uneconomical in those locations. R&D flex facilities, however, achieve higher rents and thus can absorb higher land costs. This positive relationship between the location of R&D flex facilities and higher-income areas also correlates to less-stringent zoning restrictions for these facilities. Their clean environment and the absence of heavy trucks increase their desirability. R&D flex facilities are, therefore, aligned with the office real estate sector to a certain degree in terms of geography. That alignment extends through the first three ranges of income. In fact, more than 95 percent of the Chicago sample is located in high-income areas. Their presence, however, declines in the highest range of income. This location pattern is logical for an industrial facility that resembles an office building but is not an actual member of the office sector.

In summary, R&D flex buildings require proximity to a blue-collar workforce. They face less-stringent zoning regulations than other industrial building types, however, and thus tend to be located in higher-income areas.

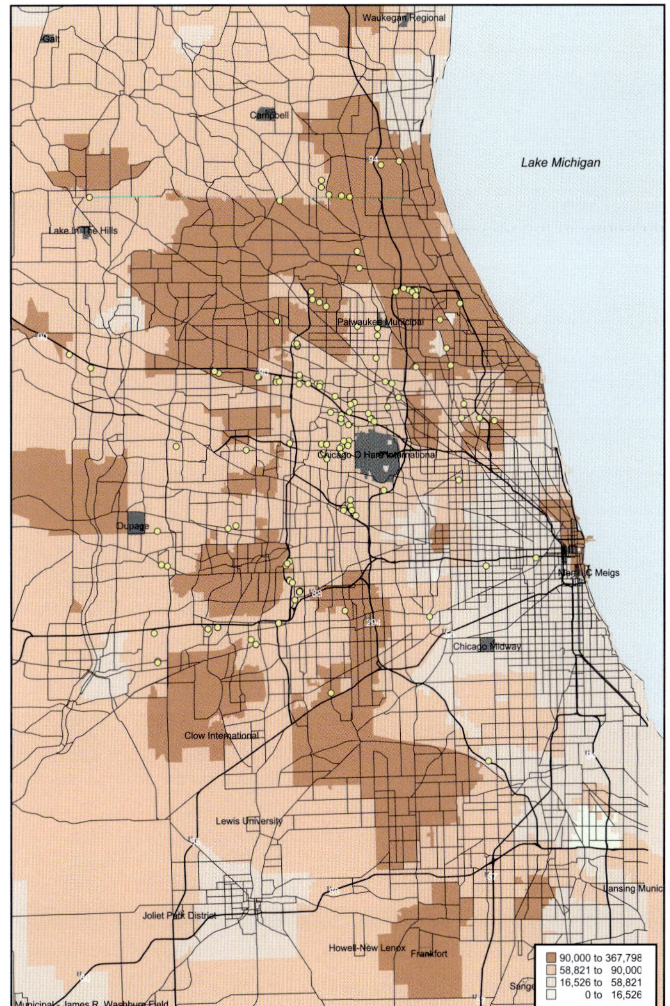

Chicago.

FLEX

OFFICE SHOWROOM

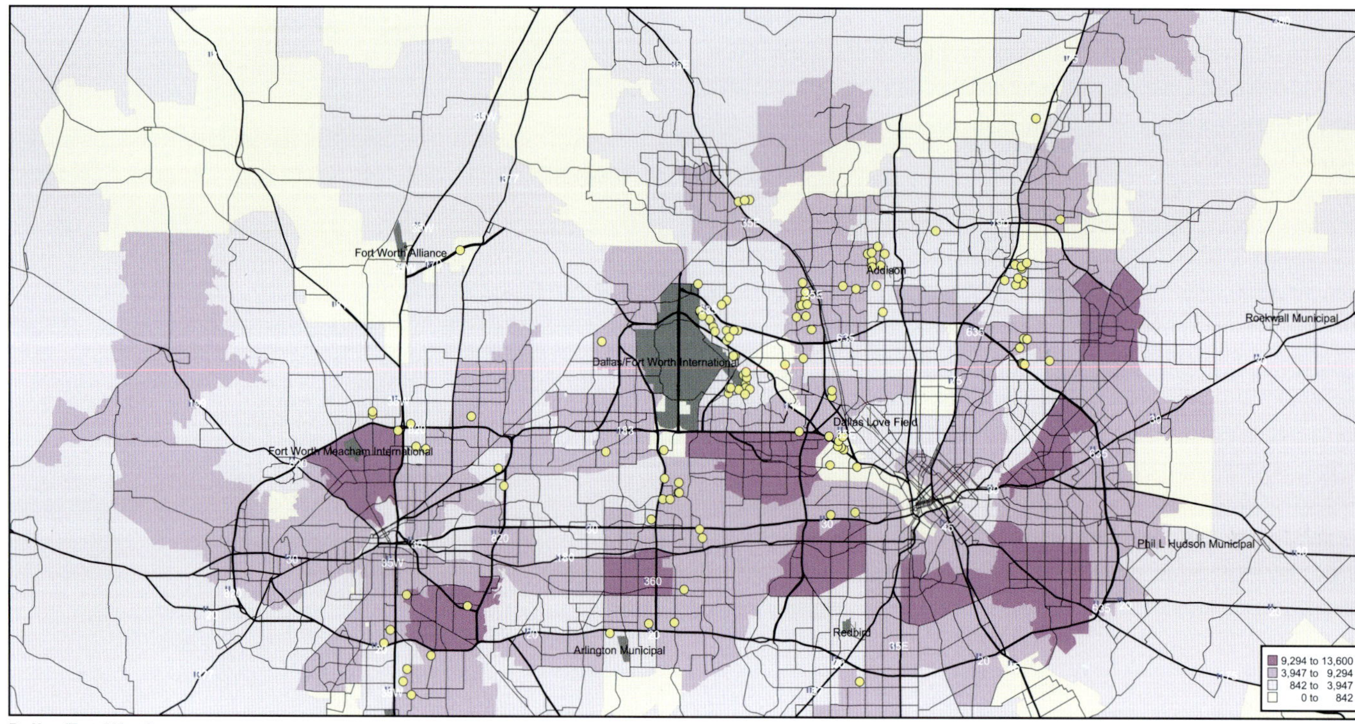

Dallas/Fort Worth.

Office showrooms and R&D flex facilities are both classified in the flex category, so similar drivers of building location could be anticipated for both, although they differ in their exterior physical attributes. The exterior of R&D flex buildings is similar to that of office buildings, whereas office showrooms bear more exterior similarity to regional warehouses. Thus, a correlation between locations of office showrooms and regional warehouses might also be expected.

The accompanying maps identify a sample of 134 office showrooms in Dallas/Fort Worth and 25 buildings in Chicago. In the Dallas/Fort Worth sample, office showrooms are located along highways and near the airport, similarly to regional warehouses. This pattern is consistent with their physical characteristics: up to 60 percent warehouse space, low ratio of square feet per loading dock, and heavy truck presence. Highway infrastructure clearly plays a central role in determining a feasible location for office showrooms.

Large concentrations of office showrooms exist in areas with a higher number of blue-collar workers. Office and showroom space account for up to 40-plus percent of the entire building, resulting in a stronger connection to labor. This attribute aligns office showrooms more closely to R&D flex facilities and the flex primary category.

Like the pattern for regional warehouses, the location of office showrooms is positively related to retail spending. About 50 percent of the sample of buildings shown on the Chicago map are located in those areas with the highest retail spending; only two facilities are located in the lowest retail spending areas; and an additional two facilities are located on the border of that area. The Chicago market pattern confirms a positive relationship between location of office showrooms and total retail spending. The sample size, however, is too limited to compare the strength of this relationship to the one identified between regional warehouses and retail spending.

In summary, the physical similarity of office showrooms to both R&D flex buildings and regional warehouses extends to a similarity with their location drivers. Highway infrastructure plays a primary role in the site selection process. In terms of demographic variables, there is a definitive positive link to total retail spending and a slightly less significant connection to the labor markets.

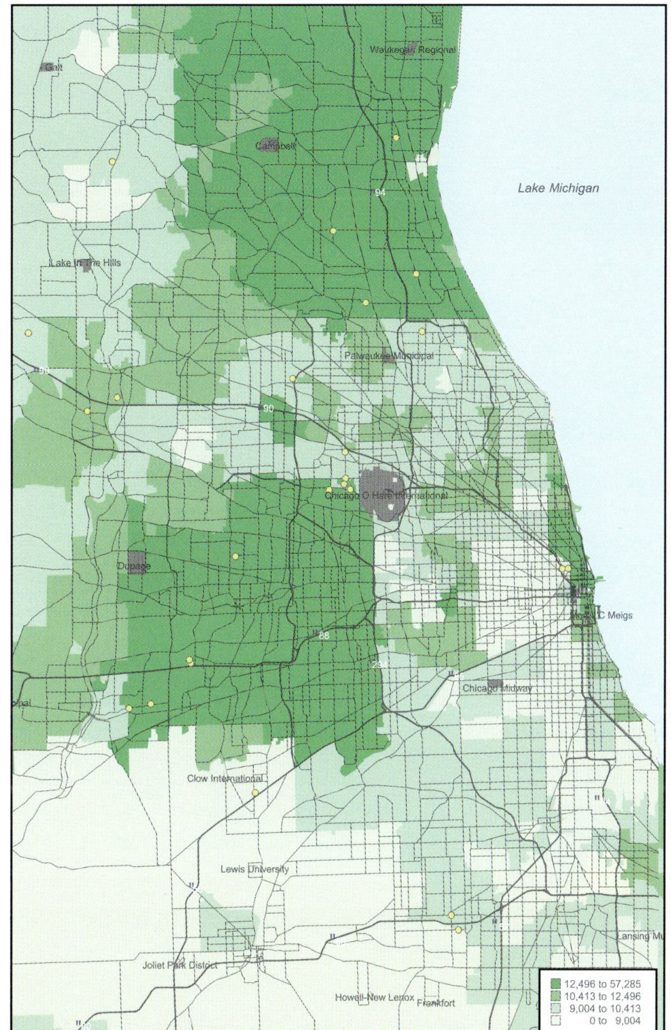

Chicago.

MULTITENANT

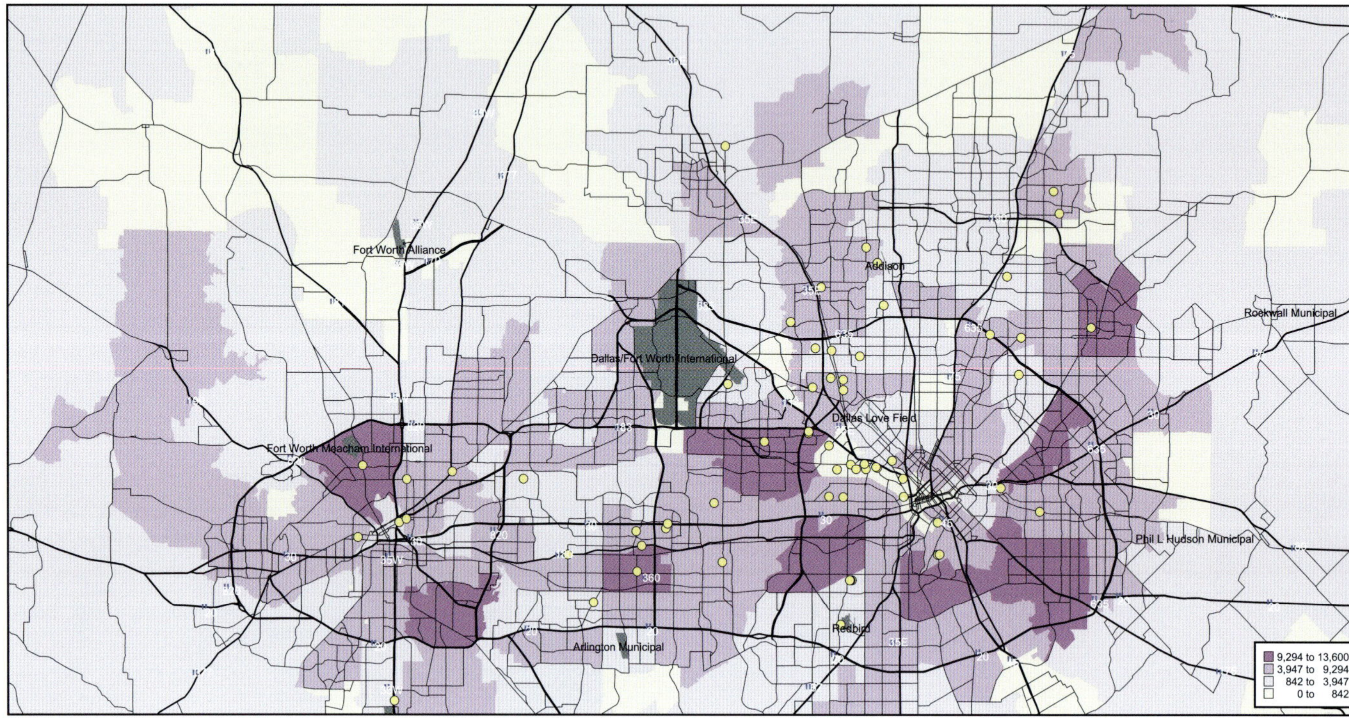

Dallas/Fort Worth.

The multitenant category is the most varied of industrial categories in terms of use and tenant base. These facilities house a variety of tenants whose requirements range from showroom to warehouse and even to light manufacturing space. The accompanying maps depict two samples of 41 and 81 multitenant buildings in the Atlanta and Dallas/Fort Worth markets, respectively.

In contrast to warehouse distribution facilities, whose primary function is distribution of goods, multitenant buildings are less dependent on direct highway access. As shown on the Dallas/Fort Worth map, they are also less likely to be located near an airport since they rarely function as distribution centers.

Multitenant buildings are smaller and have lower per square foot labor requirements than manufacturing buildings, whose primary location driver after zoning is access to labor. This difference is illustrated on the Dallas/Fort Worth map, which shows a comparable distribution of multitenant buildings across the three lowest ranges of blue-collar labor. In the highest range, the presence of multitenant buildings decreases. This pattern of even distribution across multiple ranges was confirmed in other major U.S. markets.

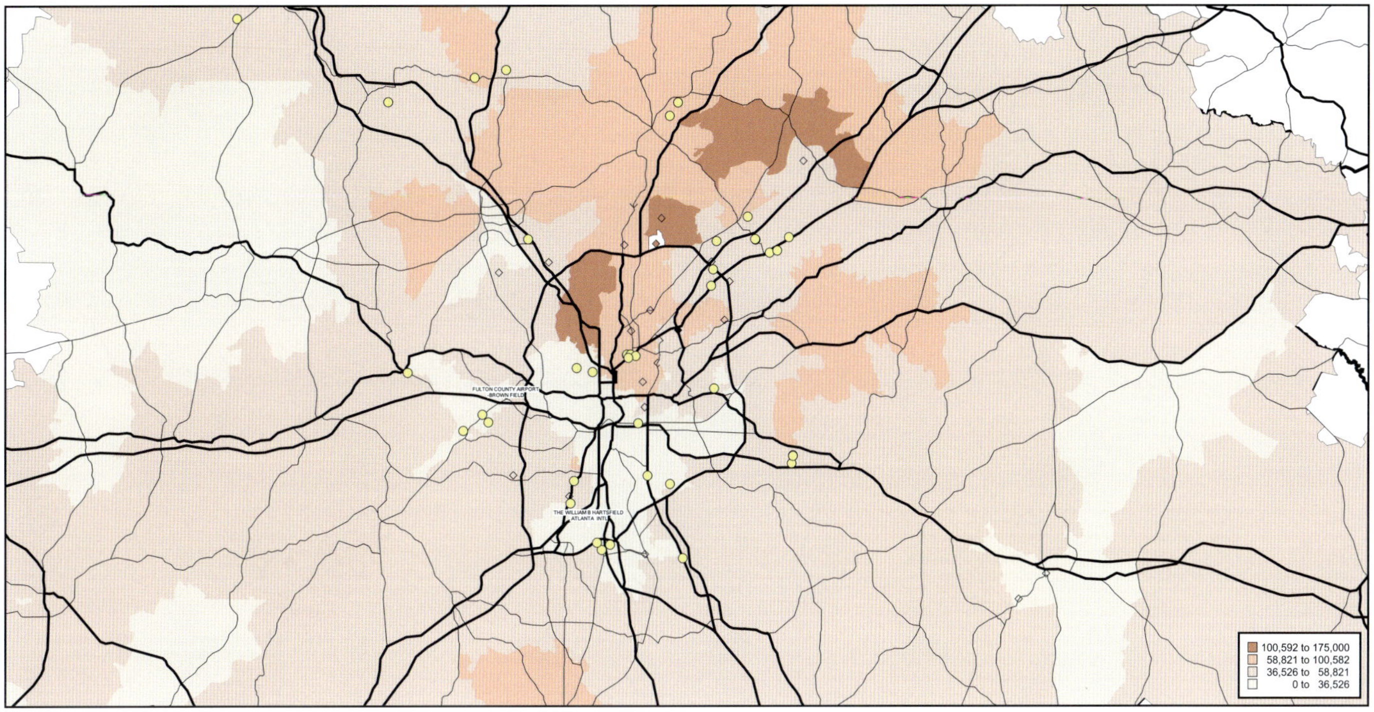

Atlanta.

Unlike R&D flex buildings, which may be located in higher-income areas with high land prices, multitenant facilities predominate in low-income areas. The Atlanta map shows the relationship between income (as a proxy for cost of land) and location of multitenant buildings. No facilities are present in the highest income range, and only 17 percent are located in the second-highest income range. This pattern is consistent across major U.S. markets. The explanation is twofold. First, tenants of multitenant buildings are commonly warehouse and light manufacturing companies. Although not to the same degree as in the case of true warehouse distribution and manufacturing buildings, such tenants do require features that result in stricter zoning restrictions. Second, multitenant buildings do not have the high finish of R&D flex buildings. Therefore, they cannot command rents that are high enough to justify the cost of land found in higher-income areas.

In summary, during site selection for multitenant buildings, zoning and land costs play a primary role. Variables that are significant for other primary types—access to highways and labor markets—play a secondary role.

FREIGHT FORWARDING

TRUCK TERMINAL

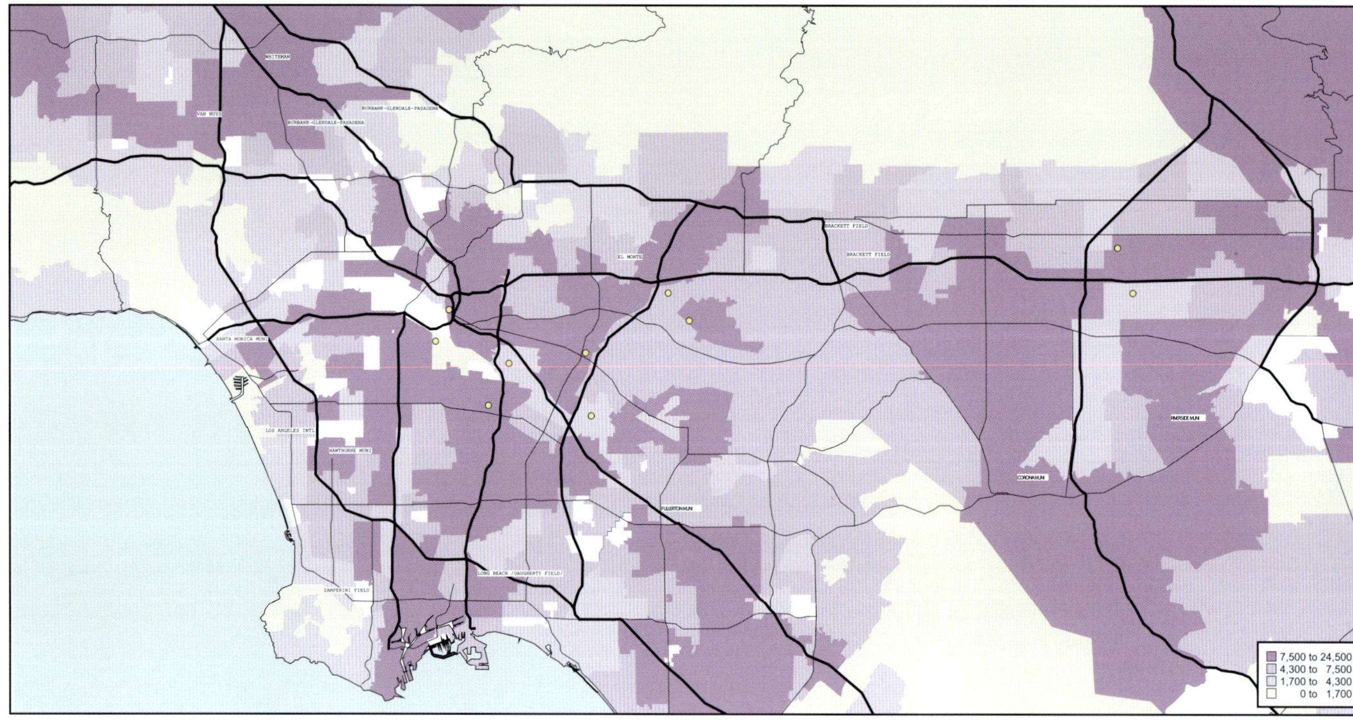

Los Angeles.

Unlike the location of air cargo buildings—which are always at airports, thus making all other location drivers immaterial—truck terminal location depends on variables such as zoning, highway infrastructure, and demographics similar to most other industrial building types. The relatively low number of truck terminals translates into a smaller sample size, as depicted on the two accompanying maps of Los Angeles. This sample size is too limited to convincingly identify location drivers, but it allows a general discussion of relevant factors.

The function of truck terminals is forwarding freight from one truck onto another truck. In response to that function, truck terminals have the lowest ratio of square feet per loading dock of all industrial types and the highest trailer-parking requirement. Access to highways plays a crucial role in location of these facilities. As a result of heavy truck traffic associated with this building type, truck terminals are subject to strict zoning restrictions and are limited to areas dominated by other industrial building types.

Access to labor is not a meaningful determinant of location. Truck terminals do not employ many workers in the absolute, nor on a per-square-foot basis. On the map of Los Angeles, the area with the smallest blue-collar workforce presence (the lightest color) has just one truck terminal. The range with the highest employment concentration (the darkest color) contains 50 percent of the sample. This seemingly strong relationship, however, is a byproduct of zoning restrictions rather than a result of labor availability.

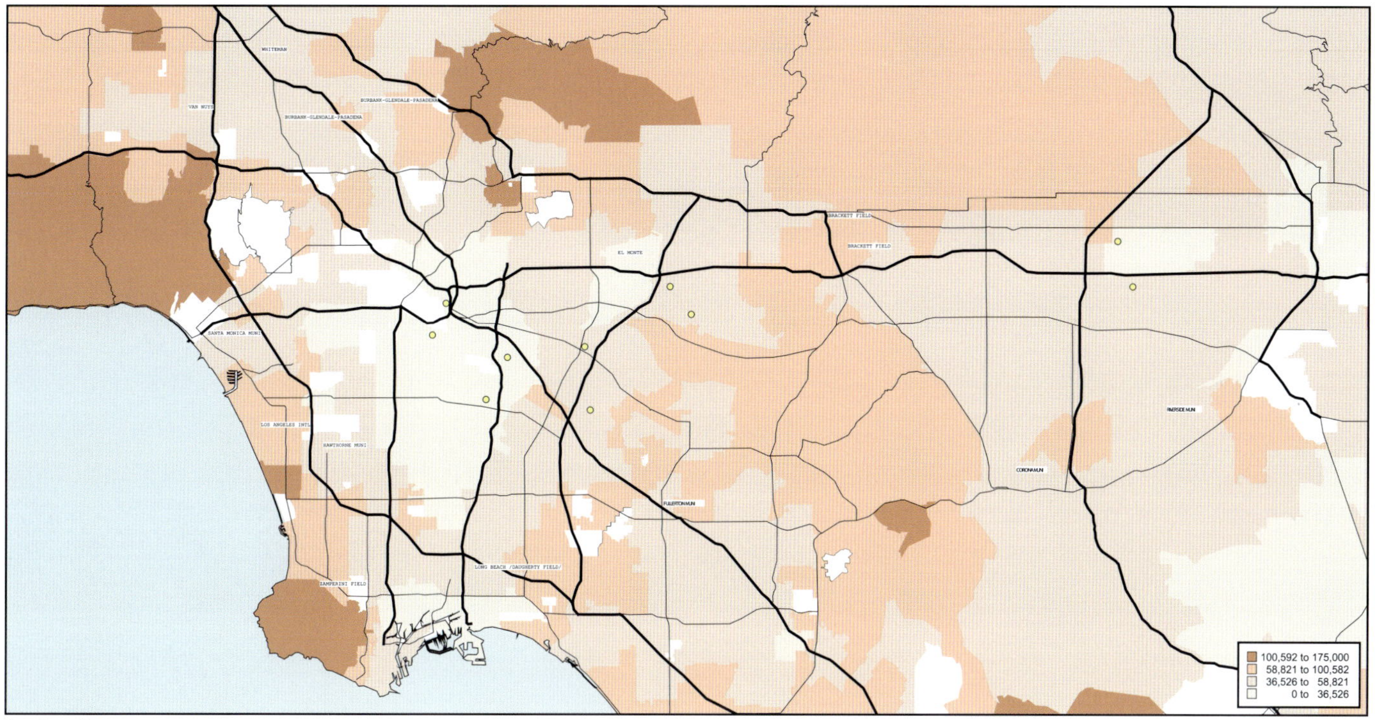

Los Angeles.

Average household income as an indicator of land price is a better guide to location than the presence of labor. All ten truck terminals on the map are located in one of the two lowest ranges of average household income. If the Denver, Chicago, and Los Angeles samples are added together, only 3 percent of truck terminals are seen to be located in high-income areas, while 60 percent are located in the lowest-income areas. Similar to the economics for other industrial types, excluding R&D flex, the cost of land is prohibitive, even if zoning is favorable.

In summary, zoning is the primary variable considered during site selection for truck terminals. After zoning, highway infrastructure plays a crucial role. Demographics have a more limited effect on location of freight-forwarding buildings than for most other industrial building types.

INVESTMENT

OVERVIEW

Compared to other sectors of real estate, the investment returns and risks of the industrial real estate sector overall have been favorable historically. As this guide illustrates, however, the physical characteristics, location, use, and tenant base of different categories of industrial real estate vary greatly and therefore have differing investment requirements and returns. The accompanying graphic identifies the variables that affect income and its valuation. Rent, occupancy levels, management expenses, recurring investments, and volatility affect income or income stream. Income stream valuation, in turn, is dependent upon an investor's investment criteria.

With regard to these variables, there are differences in investment performance for each industrial category. For example, recurring investments are lower for warehouse distribution facilities than for flex facilities. And the investments for flex facilities are lower than those for data switch centers. Additionally, rental rates for industrial properties vary according to building types. Warehouse distribution has the lowest rental rates; data switch centers have the highest. The other variables affecting income also demonstrate differing ranges of values among industrial categories.

The primary categories of industrial property have different types of owners. The owners of manufacturing and freight buildings commonly occupy their facilities. Institutional investors typically own warehouse distribution and flex buildings. Smaller private investors own more multitenant buildings. Opportunity investors, or those who speculate in investments that have much higher initial yields, own data switch centers. Despite the added risk, an even greater variety of owners exists within the secondary industrial categories.

Investment performance varies over time. For example, the investment performance of warehouse distribution facilities has varied quarterly from 1997 to 2002, both within the category and in comparison to the overall industrial-sector average. The national industrial market also demonstrates ongoing variation in investment performance.

Income Stream Valuation

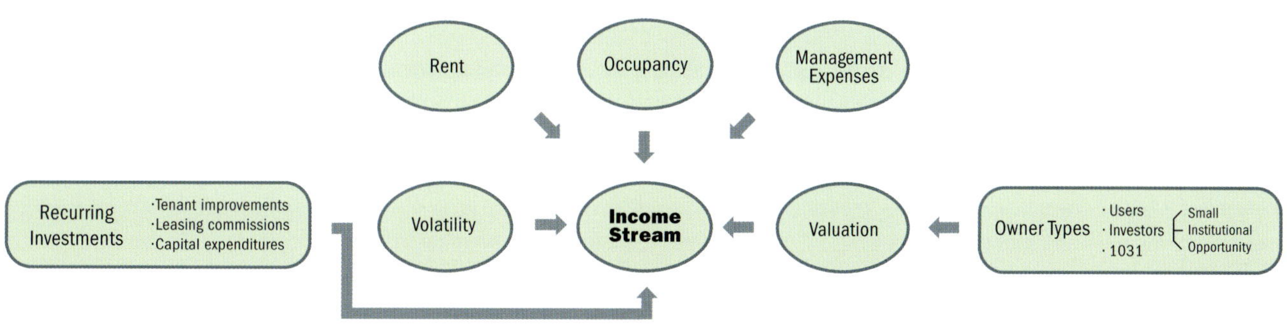

WAREHOUSE DISTRIBUTION

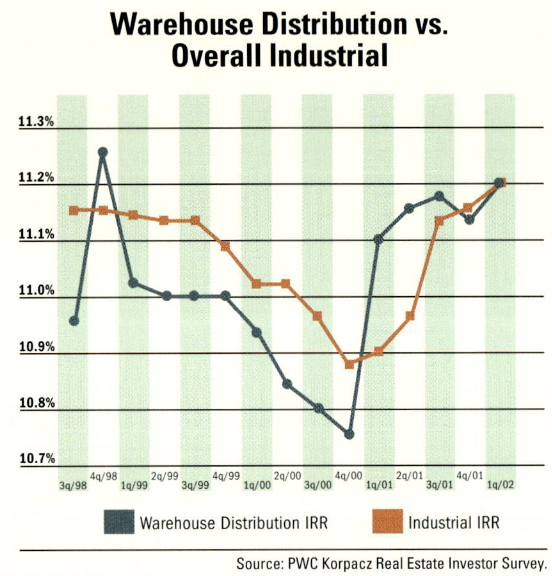

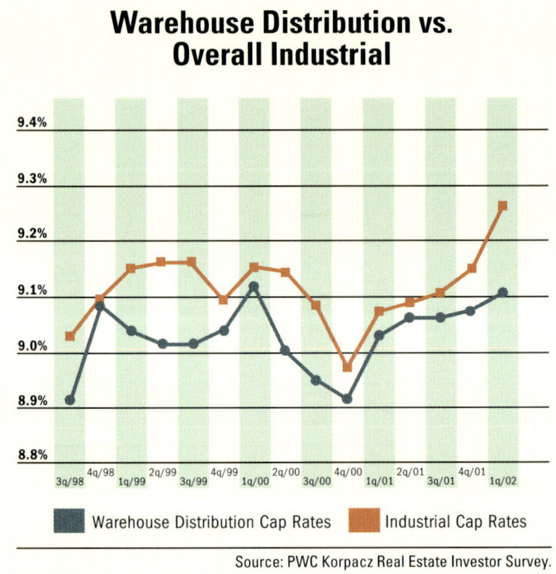

Detailed historical statistical information is readily available for warehouse distribution facilities as a result of their large market share. The accompanying graphics depict the investment performance of the warehouse distribution category from the third quarter of 1998 to the first quarter of 2002 compared with the overall industrial market. Measured by the internal rate of return (IRR), warehouse distribution buildings on average have generated lower investment returns than the overall industrial sector. Exceptions occurred at the end of 1998 and during the first three quarters of 2001, when real estate markets were affected by economic conditions and changes in the availability of capital. In general, however, warehouse distribution facilities are perceived as less risky investments. The overall capitalization rates for this facility type are consistently below those of the overall industrial sector during the same time period, which confirms the lower risk perception.

On average, warehouse distribution facilities command lower rents than the other five primary categories of industrial property. Lower rents are especially common for bulk and regional warehouses. The lower level of investment necessary to accommodate a typical tenant in these facilities justifies the lower rents. The more specialized refrigerated distribution facilities require a higher overall investment and, therefore, command higher rents.

Because warehouse distribution facilities have low retrofit costs and are easy to re-lease, tenants can easily relocate to a different building that has lower rents. For that reason warehouse distribution facilities—excluding rack-supported buildings—are commoditylike, or easily substitutable, and sensitive to price, which keeps rents relatively low. Because of their specific racking size and weight constraints, rack-supported facilities rarely can be re-leased.

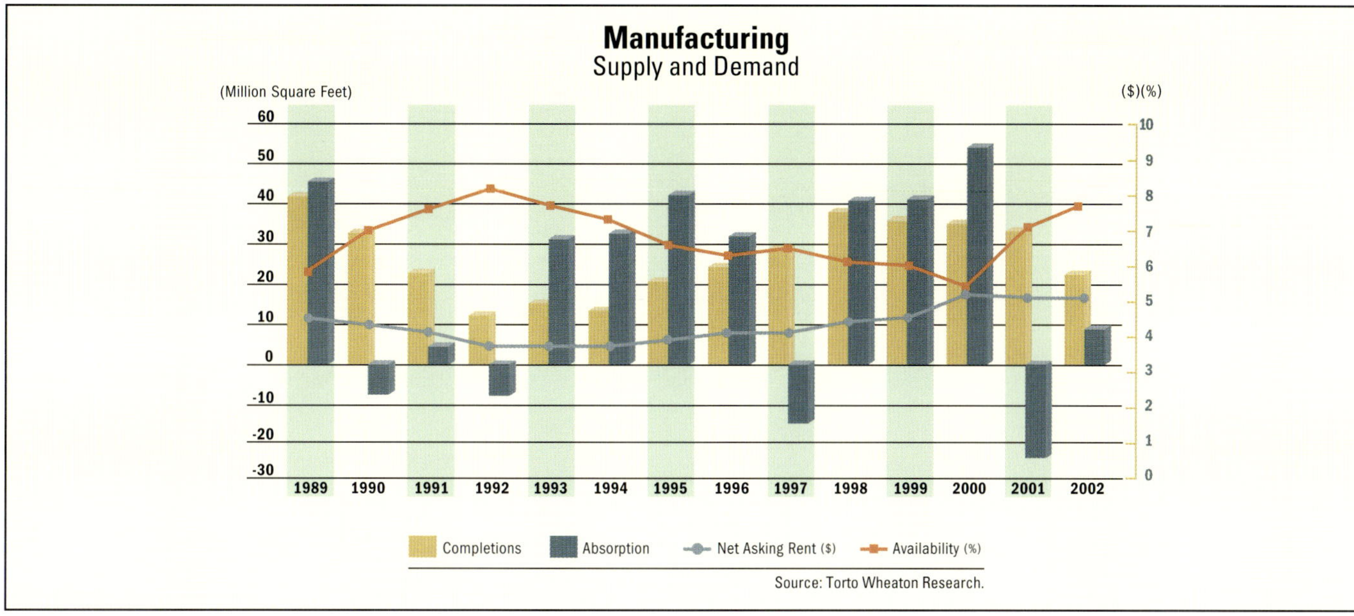

Manufacturing
Supply and Demand

Although manufacturing buildings historically have been classified and tracked, most facilities are owner-occupied, which reduces the available performance data on income and investment. Owners who also are the buildings' users value real estate differently from investors, complicating the comparison.

Supply and demand data for manufacturing facilities, on the contrary, are readily available. The accompanying graph depicts the construction completion and net absorption totals for these facilities from 1989 to 2002. The national availability rate for manufacturing declined between 1992 and 2000, with a minor rise in 1997, after which construction outpaced absorption. In 2001, net absorption turned negative as a response to a manufacturing recession, pushing availability rates back up to their 1993 levels by the end of 2000.

One trend not captured by the graph is the declining market share of manufacturing facilities within the United States, which results from the increasing relocation of American plants to foreign countries to take advantage of cheaper labor. Between 1992 and 2001, the total square footage of manufacturing facilities in the United States increased by only 8.2 percent. In contrast, the square footage of warehouse distribution and flex facilities grew by 20.1 percent and 21.3 percent, respectively.

Investment in tenant improvements is greater for manufacturing facilities than for warehouse distribution buildings, but less so than in flex buildings. This type of investment not only increases average rents, but also increases retrofit costs and, therefore, the overall risk involved. In contrast, because of high tenant-relocation costs, the tenant retention of manufacturing facilities is higher, and leases are longer.

FLEX

Flex vs. Overall Industrial

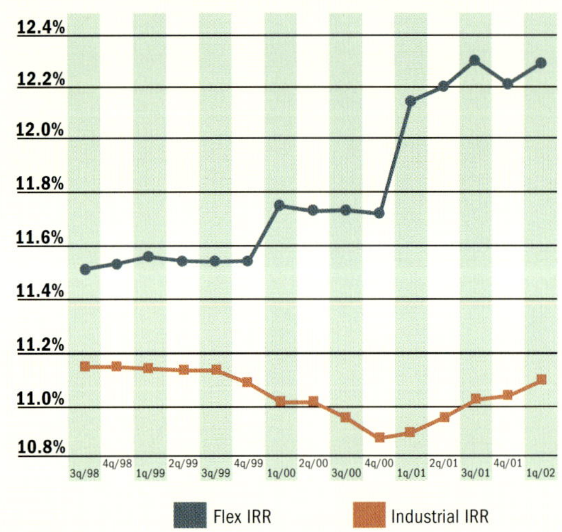

Source: PWC Korpacz Real Estate Investor Survey.

Flex vs. Overall Industrial

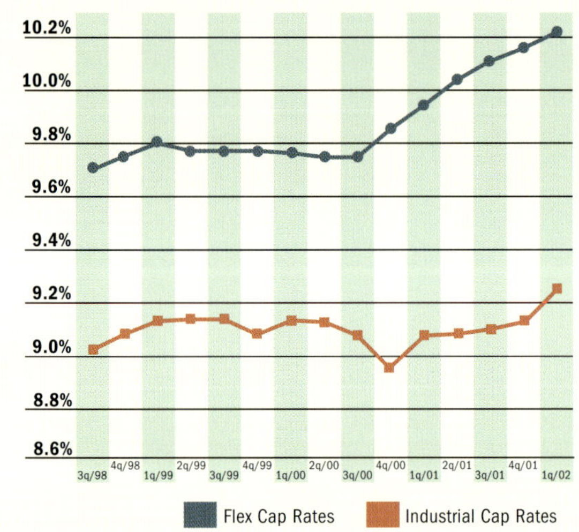

Source: PWC Korpacz Real Estate Investor Survey.

Along with warehouse distribution and manufacturing, flex is one of the most widely tracked of industrial categories. Flex facilities are more commonly owned by investors, which results in availability of better investment and performance data. The accompanying graphs depict the investment performance of flex facilities from third quarter 1998 to first quarter 2002. Two noticeable trends are indicated. First, flex facilities command a higher rate of return on investment than the overall industrial sector. Second, the difference in performance for flex facilities varies over time. With respect to IRR, during 1999 the spread between flex and overall industrial was 38 basis points lower than in 1997, which in turn was 38 basis points lower than in 2001. The better-than-average performance of flex facilities is confirmed in the figure depicting overall capitalization rates.

The higher return on investment for flex facilities results from their level of risk, which varies over time. The change in level of risk is evident from the increase in investment return in 2000 and the first half of 2001. During 2000, flex buildings increasingly became cheaper alternatives to office buildings for start-up technology or dot-com companies. These businesses typically have low or nonexistent credit, leading to a higher level of liability requiring a higher investment return. Required investment per square foot is also higher compared to warehouse distribution and manufacturing buildings, which further increases the risk. The higher investment is necessary because flex buildings are located in higher-income areas, where land is more expensive and construction materials are higher quality and costly. Also, more tenant improvements are required, especially for R&D flex facilities.

Multitenant vs. Industrial Market
Midyear 2001 Availability Rate

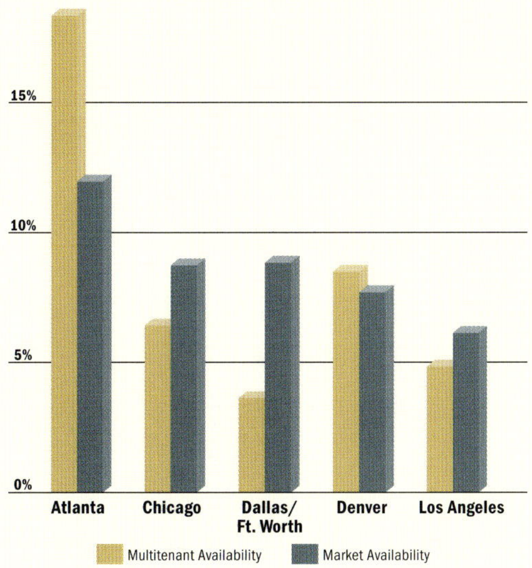

Source: CoStar Group.

Multitenant vs. Industrial Market
Midyear 2001 Asking Gross Rents

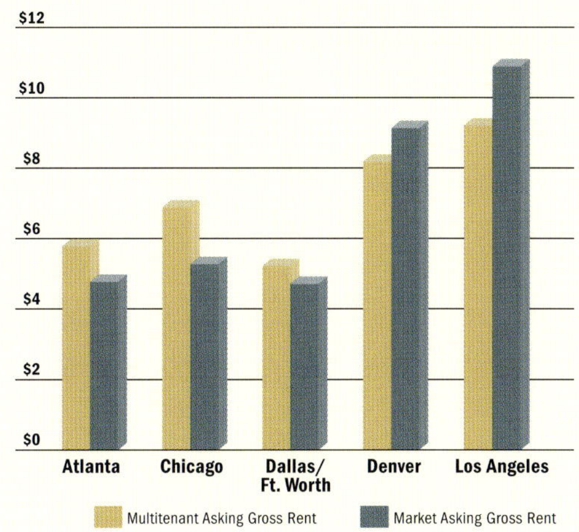

Source: CoStar Group.

Because multitenant facilities historically have not been classified as a separate category, historical investment and market data are lacking. The accompanying graphs depict multitenant availability and rental rates in five major industrial real estate markets. The availability rate for this category is higher than the overall industrial rate in two markets (Atlanta and Denver), and lower in the other three (Chicago, Dallas, and Los Angeles). On the whole, the availability rate for multitenant facilities in the second quarter of 2001 was 7.4 percent, which is 110 basis points lower than the overall five-market industrial rate of 8.5 percent. On average, the asking gross rents are slightly higher than the average rents for all industrial types combined. Among the primary industrial categories, the rents of multitenant buildings are higher than those of warehouse distribution buildings but below the levels of flex buildings.

The level of tenant improvements for multitenant facilities is sufficiently high for the buildings not to be perceived as commoditylike, but not high enough to prevent tenants from relocating. Retrofit costs and re-leasing difficulties are moderate. These variables result in investment returns for multitenant facilities that are higher than those of bulk warehouses but below the investment returns of R&D flex buildings.

FREIGHT FORWARDING

Both truck terminals and air cargo buildings are primarily owner-occupied, which limits available data. The low number of total freight facilities in existence also precludes solid availability and rental data. For these reasons, there are no national income and market data for the freight-forwarding industrial category. General observations can be made, however, with respect to variables that affect this category's investment performance.

Trucking companies are the typical tenants of truck terminals. These tenants generally have lower credit, which results in a higher level of risk and increased capitalization rates. The capitalization rates for truck terminals typically range from 10 to 13 percent. The rates are lower in major freight-forwarding markets, such as Chicago and Los Angeles, and higher in secondary and tertiary markets, which have riskier tenants.

Truck terminals and air cargo buildings are designed for a specific use, which reduces the feasibility of retrofit without major redevelopment. That, in turn, makes re-leasing opportunities more limited for these types of facilities.

Freight facilities have a unique market characteristic. Quoted rents and overall valuation, particularly for truck terminals, are made on a per door, rather than a per square foot, basis. Because of this different valuation, it is difficult to correctly compare the market statistics of such facilities with the other five primary industrial categories. Although rental rates and valuations that are per door can be converted to per square foot, the converted numbers are of little value because they were initially derived on a per door basis.

DATA SWITCH CENTER

Because data switch center is the newest category of industrial real estate, little national historical investment and performance data are available. However, a unique characteristic of these facilities is their dual, or two-time, availability rate. The facility is first leased to tenants referred to as data warehousers. Those tenants then lease individual cages to other companies. Therefore, when a data switch center is initially leased, it remains available for sublease. Because of this dual availability rate, it is difficult to predict future demand.

From an investment perspective, the data switch center primary category is also too new to have an efficient market. It was an owners' market during 2000 because a typical tenant's investment in equipment exceeded the rental payment to such a degree that a facility's owner could impose virtually any rent. That held especially true if the owner could meet the tenant's immediate timetable. An entirely different situation has unfolded during 2001. Along with the financial markets, the telecommunications market has experienced significant volatility and upheaval. In fact, many data warehousing companies have disappeared, leaving vacant buildings. This degree of volatility is indicative of market inefficiencies.

In general, investment in tenant improvements is the highest for data switch center facilities among all categories of industrial real estate. Moreover, most data switch center tenants are new companies without credit history. They are considered risky, which justifies higher returns. Over time this market will become more efficient, which will stabilize investment returns. However, of the industrial categories, data switch center is likely to remain the riskiest investment, thus commanding the highest rates of return.

SUPPLY CHAIN

SUPPLY CHAIN

Supply chain, or the process of moving goods from a beginning to an end point, is an integral part of industrial real estate. Supply chain is simply a sequence of events intended to satisfy customers who require products. In order to reach consumers, products need to be manufactured (created), then stored, and finally sold (distributed). The three processes that form the supply chain—manufacturing, storage, and distribution—each require specific types of industrial real estate. Distribution, the final process in the supply chain, also requires a retail component. An understanding of the supply chain is fundamental to the classification of industrial real estate because it explains why the various types of industrial facilities exist, how they function and interact, and how they may evolve.

A traditional industrial supply chain is depicted in the accompanying graphic showing the three processes of the supply chain: creation of goods, storage, and distribution. Factory icons represent the creation of goods. Warehouses represent their storage. Houses represent the customers. The lines that connect the individual icons represent the distribution of these goods. Only two industrial property types are depicted in the chain leading to the consumer: manufacturing and warehouse distribution.

It would be difficult to construct a supply chain graphic that incorporated all industrial property types. The supply chains of different industries use different property types. Not every property type plays a role in every industry's supply chain. For example, a furniture manufacturer would not need a refrigerated distribution facility in its production and distribution scheme. In the case of more complex industrial supply chains, however, many types of properties may be necessary. Bulk warehouses, which store and distribute a variety of raw, intermediate, and finished goods, could be placed between each column of factories in the graphic, indicating different stages of manufacture. The same applies to distribution and freight-forwarding facilities, such as heavy distribution facilities, truck terminals, and air cargo buildings, in which goods are typically sorted, stored, and shipped. In the graphic, these property types would be placed between the columns representing Subassembly Manufacturing and Final Assembly Manufacturing.

Traditional Industrial Supply Chain

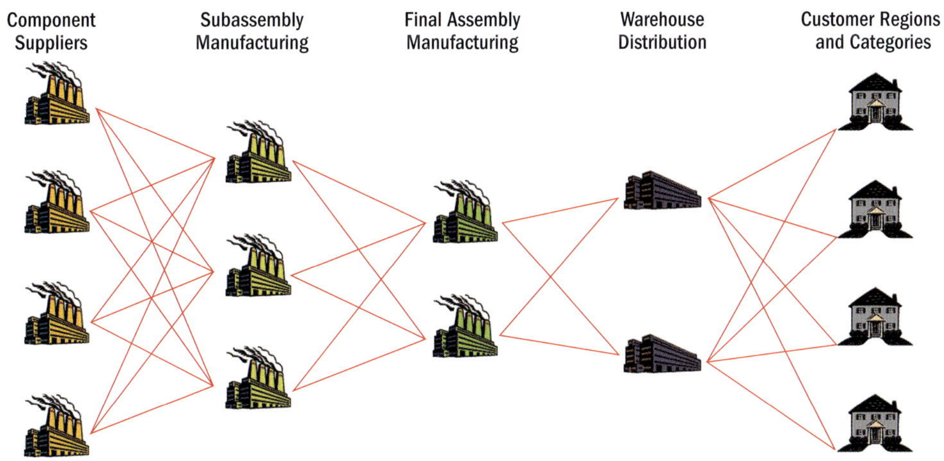

SUPPLY CHAIN

In addition, each of the three columns of factories depicted could be further subdivided into several interacting manufacturing and warehouse distribution buildings that, in collaboration, accomplish the production steps. A more visually practical supply chain graphic would be one focusing on the three processes of creating, storing, and distributing. The graphic below places each of the 12 secondary industrial categories and two unsubdivided primary categories within these supply chain processes of creation, storage, and distribution.

Certain industrial property types are best suited to fulfill one process only, whereas other property types are sufficiently flexible in physical characteristics to accommodate multiple processes. For example, the sole function of truck terminals is to forward freight. Bulk warehouses can store and distribute goods. In multitenant buildings, the three functions of manufacturing, storage, and distribution may be performed within the same facility. Allocating all six primary and 12 secondary industrial property types among these three principal supply chain functions demonstrates why such a variety of building types is needed in a classification system.

Data switch centers are positioned as a separate circle in the second graphic. These newer industrial facilities are unique in that they do not create, store, or distribute. Rather, they provide information technology (IT) network support to businesses, a new function that is emerging within modern industrial real estate supply chains.

Property Categories in the Supply Chain

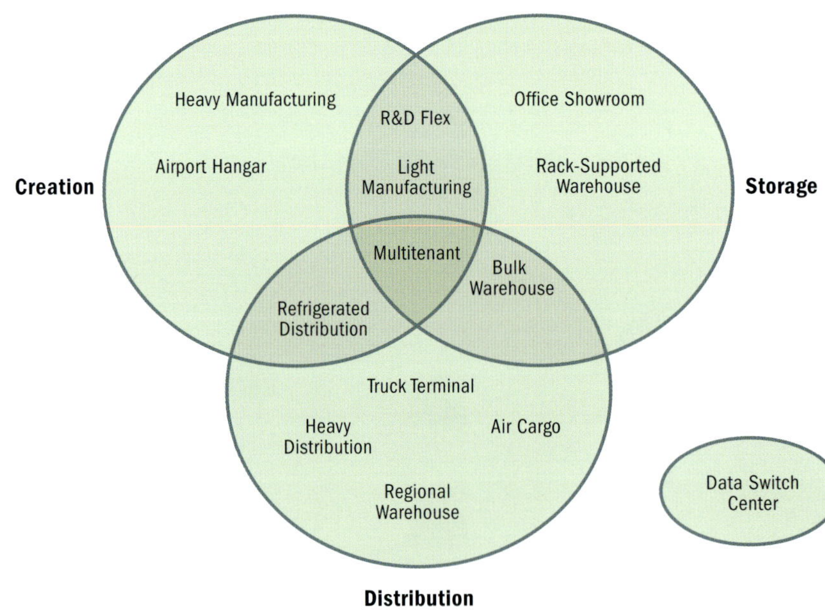

SUPPLY CHAIN

Modern industrial real estate supply chains are evolving. In fact, there are two major trends: (1) a growing focus by companies on their core competencies, or specialized lines of business, instead of peripheral activities; and (2) the combining of functions within physical structures.

With regard to the first trend, corporations are moving away from a linear—or start-to-finish—integration, in which they own and perform all activities. Instead, businesses are moving toward a radial, or collaborative, integration, in which they focus only on their specialized lines of work and outsource the remainder. Although this trend affects the ownership of individual buildings within a particular supply chain, the actual supply chain does not change. For example, when Ford Motor Company spun off Visteon Corporation, the owner of some manufacturing plants changed from Ford to Visteon. The plants, however, were not removed from Ford's supply chain; instead, they were added to the new owner's supply chain. The evolutionary trend of radial integration, therefore, does not affect the life of industrial property types. The accompanying graphic depicts the historical linear supply chain as well as the evolving collaborative one.

Linear Supply Chain

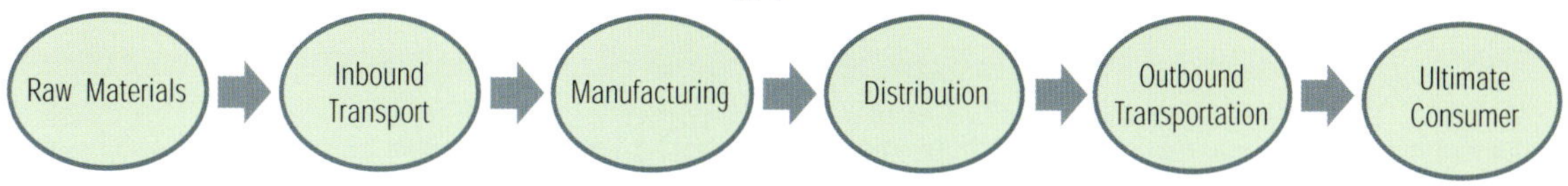

Collaborative Supply Chain

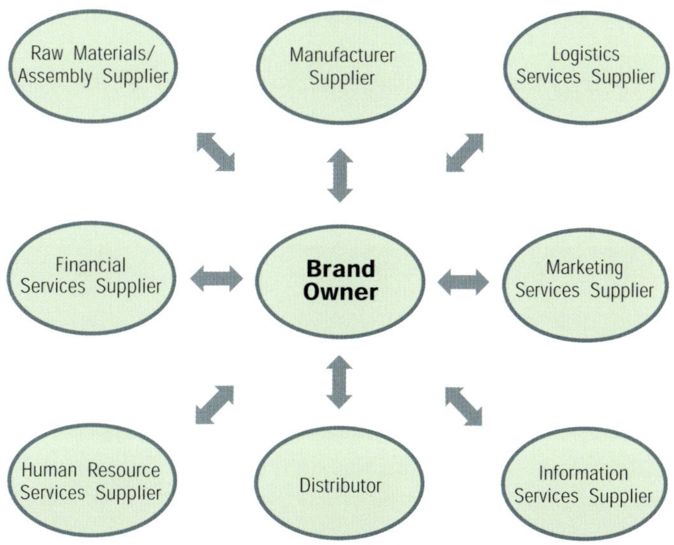

SUPPLY CHAIN

A second major trend affecting the evolution of the supply chain is the combining of processes within the same industrial facility for the purpose of reducing overall costs. Dell Computer Corporation transformed a traditional warehouse into a facility that assembles and distributes directly to its customers, combining the manufacturing, warehousing, and distribution processes and thus eliminating the need for two separate industrial facility types (manufacturing plant and warehouse distribution facility). Applying this example to the second accompanying graphic, a typical bulk warehouse is categorized within the union of storage and distribution circles. Dell Computer Corporation, however, moved this property type into the intersection of all three circles (creation, storage, and distribution) when it combined the three processes.

Will the evolution in industrial supply chains affect future classification methods of industrial real estate? It should not affect classification of industrial real estate by physical characteristics. Those industrial processes that can be combined for cost-saving reasons are physically compatible and can be performed in buildings with similar physical characteristics. For example, light manufacturing activities can be combined with bulk warehouse or heavy distribution activities in the same facility because buildings housing these functions are similar in physical characteristics, with only a few distinguishing features. Buildings suited to functions that require substantially different physical characteristics, however, cannot be combined—for example, facilities for heavy manufacturing and R&D flex. The former are very large and geared to heavy-duty production. The latter have a distinctive officelike atmosphere and a cleaner environment. Moreover, if the defining ranges of industrial facility types are expanded because of technological advances or supply chain evolution, physical characteristics can still classify buildings. For example, technological advances are driving ceiling heights higher in modern warehouse distribution buildings. By expanding the defining ceiling height range in a physical classification process, these buildings still fit well into the warehouse distribution primary category.

In summary, industrial real estate plays a vital and integral role in fulfilling supply chain management. Manufacturing, storage, and distribution are the three principal uses of industrial real estate. Goods need to be manufactured, stored, and distributed to customers. These functions demand specific types of industrial structures, which results in a variety of industrial real estate property types and justifies the classification of industrial real estate by physical characteristics. Advances in supply chain management are resulting in changes in the use of specific building types, as well as in their physical characteristics. By expanding the defining ranges, these changes can be readily accommodated within a physical classification system.

GLOSSARY

GLOSSARY

Absorption: Change in occupied space.

Ampere: A unit of electric current equal to the steady current produced by one volt acting through a resistance of one ohm.

Ancillary differentiating feature: A feature that is common in industrial buildings of the same category but not always present (for example, trailer parking is common but not always present in heavy distribution buildings).

Availability rate: Available space divided by total existing space.

Available space: Space available for occupancy. It includes both vacant space and occupied space that is being marketed and will become vacant by the end of the reporting period.

Average household income: The average of all income earned (wages, salaries, fringe benefits, profit, rent, interest, etc.) and transfer benefits (social security, unemployment compensation, welfare), minus social security taxes paid to the government.

Blue-collar worker: Of or relating to wage earners, especially as a class whose jobs often involve manual labor and are performed in work clothes.

Build-to-suit (BTS): A property built or altered by the landlord to the specifications of the tenant.

Cap rate: Initial rate of return in an all-cash transaction.

Core differentiating feature: A feature that is consistently present in all industrial buildings within the same category (for example, multiple docks are always present in truck terminals).

Correlation: A relationship between two variables.

Cross dock: Loading docks situated along two parallel walls.

Curb appeal: A building's external physical appearance, as affected by landscaping, materials, exterior roads, and the like. R&D flex buildings have the highest curb appeal of industrial facilities; heavy manufacturing buildings have the lowest curb appeal.

Drive-in door: A door through which a truck enters a facility for the purpose of loading.

Exterior features: The principal physical characteristics used to classify buildings from the outside: building size, site coverage, loading capability, car and trailer parking, and so forth.

Exterior loading dock: A loading platform accessible from the building's exterior at which trucks park for the purposes of loading and unloading.

Floor levelness: The degree of floor flatness; an important variable associated with buildings that have high ceilings.

Floor load: The amount of weight that a floor surface can support measured in pounds per square inch (PSI), assuming a uniformly distributed load.

Heavy power: A term used in association with buildings that require an above average amount of power (for example, manufacturing buildings).

HVAC: Heating, ventilation, and air conditioning.

Income valuation: Estimation of a property's value based on the premise that the value of the real estate is equal to the present worth of the anticipated future income stream.

Interior features: The principal physical characteristics used to classify buildings from the inside: ceiling heights, space buildout, power, floor load, and so forth.

Interior loading dock: A loading platform located inside the building structure at which trucks park for the purposes of loading and unloading.

GLOSSARY

Intermodal freight forwarding: Transport of goods from one mode to another (for example, from truck to airplane).

Internal rate of return (IRR): Discount rate in an all-cash transaction, based on annual year-end compounding.

Intramodal freight forwarding: Transport of goods within the same mode (for example, from truck to truck).

Linear integration (Vertical integration): Ownership of operations at different and usually sequential levels of supply chain that range from processing raw materials to distribution to end customers.

Management expenses: Costs associated with the management of a property.

Mezzanine office: An office buildout on an intermediate floor that does not have the same area as the bottom floor.

North American Industry Classification System (NAICS): The classification of establishments by the type of activity in which they are engaged; utilized for purposes of facilitating the collection, tabulation, presentation, and analysis of data, and for promoting uniformity and comparability in the presentation of statistical data collected by various agencies of the United States, Canadian, and Mexican governments. [Source: U.S. Office of Management and Budget, *North American Industry Classification System* (Washington, D.C.: U.S. Office of Management and Budget, 1997).]

Occupancy rate: Occupied space divided by total existing space.

Ordinal numbers: A number system that measures the order or position instead of the value or amount.

Owner-occupied: Facility that is occupied by the owner.

Parking requirement: The minimum number of parking spaces required by a tenant; usually provided as a ratio per 1,000 square feet (for example, 1 to 1,000 square feet).

Primary category: A category that encompasses certain industrial buildings based on major physical characteristics, such as loading and space buildout.

Radial integration: Ownership of core operations and outsourcing of supporting operations of supply chain.

Recurring investment: Repeating investment in a building for purposes of leasing, tenant improvements, and leasing commissions; maintenance; and capital expenditures.

Retrofit costs: Costs associated with improving a property through rehabilitation, modernization, and remodeling for the purpose of re-leasing.

Sample: A section of the total population used to derive information for that entire population.

Secondary category: A category that encompasses certain buildings based on more detailed physical characteristics with specific ranges and ratios. Physical characteristics include size, space buildout, loading, and the like.

Site coverage: Percentage of total site dedicated to the physical building structure; usually reported as a percentage or ratio. Site coverage of 50 percent, or a ratio of 2 to 1, indicates that 50 percent of the entire site is covered by the physical structure. The remaining 50 percent is usually dedicated to truck courts, car and trailer parking, and landscaping.

Space buildout: A physical arrangement of space within a building. The major types of space arrangement within industrial buildings include warehouse, manufacturing/assembly, repair, lab/high tech, and office.

Supply chain: A network of facilities and distribution options that procures materials, transforms these materials into intermediate and finished products, and distributes these finished products to customers. Supply chains exist in both service and manufacturing organizations, although the complexity of the chain may vary greatly from industry to industry and firm to firm. [Source: Ganeshan, Ram, and Terry P. Harrison, *An Introduction to Supply Chain Management* (Pennsylvania State University); http://silmaril.smeal.psu.edu/misc/supply_chain_intro.html.]

Tenant improvements allowance: An allowance provided to tenants as a concession to improve and/or build out space to their specifications.

Total retail spending: Total dollars spent by consumers on merchandise that is sold by establishments primarily engaged in retail trade.

Truck court: An area along a building's dock doors comprising the loading and truck maneuvering areas.

Underwriting: The process of estimating and verifying property's cash flow.

Volt: The practical unit of electromotive force; the difference of potential capable of sending a current of one ampere through a conductor whose resistance is one ohm.

Watt: A unit of electric power equal to the power in a circuit in which a current of one ampere flows across a potential difference of one volt [Watts = Volts x Amperes].

Zoning: Regulation of private land use and development by local government.